KW-360-260

Contents

About the author

Brian Fahy was born in 1947 of a Lancashire father and an Irish mother. For many years he was a priest in a Catholic preaching order, the Redemptorists. He met and married Maggie, and they have a son, Michael. Maggie died suddenly in 2012. Brian writes homilies and Christian articles for publication, and also practises as a family mediator with Relationships Scotland, helping separating parents make good arrangements for their children. Brian is a lifelong supporter of Bolton Wanderers, and has a lifelong love of the West of Ireland.

www.kevinmayhew.com

KM PUBLISHING

First published in Great Britain in 2013 by Kevin Mayhew Ltd
Buxhall, Stowmarket, Suffolk IP14 3BW
Tel: +44 (0) 1449 737978 Fax: +44 (0) 1449 737834
E-mail: info@kevinmayhewltd.com

www.kevinmayhew.com

Scripture quotations are taken from *The Jerusalem Bible*, Darton, Longman &
Todd Ltd, 1966.

9 8 7 6 5 4 3 2 1 0

ISBN 978 1 84867 661 9
Catalogue No. 1501409

Cover design by Rob Mortonson
© Images used under licence from Shutterstock Inc.
Edited by Nicki Copeland
Typeset by Richard Weaver

Printed and bound in Great Britain

Introduction

After my previous book, *Finding Maggie*, was accepted for publication,[1] I realised that there were some stories still waiting and wanting to be told. Like girls sitting around the edge of a dance floor, waiting for someone to invite them up to dance, these stories are only waiting to be asked. I invite you to join them now, and to see for yourself how well they can dance!

Lots of the stories follow the long line of my mother's life – she lived for 94 years! In snippets and snapshots I want to tell of her life, for it is the background to my own, and I want to weave the thread of my own story in and out of my mother's, for that is what our lives are really like.

The central thread of my own story is presented here. I was encouraged away from home at the age of 11 to train for the Catholic priesthood. I was in a religious order for 41 years, in priesthood for 29. Eventually I left it all and joined myself to Maggie and to my son, Michael. I would like it to be known that this was not a dereliction of duty but a walk into freedom, even a long walk to freedom, if I may borrow Nelson Mandela's famous phrase.

There are lessons here for the learning, and not too late for the learning. Much as I love my faith and my Church, it would be a dereliction of devotion not to point out errors and mistakes when they occur. It is not a sign of true love to close our eyes to faults and failings in the one we love. But, in these pages, I would like the story to do

---

1. *Finding Maggie* (Kevin Mayhew, 2013).

the talking, and the lessons, whatever they may be, to arise gently from the page.

In the course of my life, many people have influenced and affected me, and generally for the good. In that simple fact alone, I am greatly blessed. But, as you will discover in these pages, two women have been powerful factors in the run of my life. The first is my mother, born Ellen Rose Carey in Glencullen, County Mayo, whose love and devotion still nourish my life, though she is now gone to God. The second is Maggie, a Dublin-born Scots lassie, the girl I met and fell in love with, the girl who patiently waited for me, the mother of my son. Maggie, too, has now gone to God, and waits for me there.

These are the women whose love for me has brought me to this day. In writing something of my own story, it has been my joy and my privilege to write something of theirs. I hope these stories dance well and bring joy and inspiration to your life, for we are all on the one road. Sometimes, as that old Irish rebel song suggests, we feel that we are 'on the road to God knows where'![2] I often felt that way. But my road led me to Maggie and to the freedom of these years.

We're on the one road.

---

2. Frank O'Donovan, 'On the one road' (1941).

ONE

A mother's love

A mother's love's a blessing
no matter where you roam.
Keep her while she's living;
you'll miss her when she's gone.
Love her as in childhood,
though feeble, old and grey,
for you'll never miss a mother's love
'til she's buried beneath the clay.[3]

I stood in front of the audience of my fellow pupils and sang this song during my first Christmas term away from home. I was 11 years old, and it was the night of the school concert. Soon we would return home for the Christmas holidays, when I would see my mother again. It had been three months since I left my Lancashire home and come to this junior college, this minor seminary, in Birmingham.

Boys between the ages of 11 and 17 who showed an interest in becoming a priest were encouraged away from their homes and families to come and live within the confines of a college and to be trained in the ways of their religion. The particular college that encouraged me away from my home and family was called Erdington Abbey, and it belonged to a preaching Order known as the Redemptorists. That college is a girls' school today. Would that it had been so back in 1958!

---

3. Thomas P. Keenan, 'A mother's love's a blessing'.

I missed my mother, just as I missed all the other members of my family – my dad, my two sisters, my little brother and my collie dog, called Bruce. Singing this Irish song, 'A mother's love's a blessing', was my natural party piece. I had been listening to it, and to many more Irish songs, on our impressive radiogram at home in our dining room from the moment I could hear.

Every year, when we came home to Tyldesley, the coalmining, cotton-mill town in Lancashire, from our happy holiday in the West of Ireland, Mammy would bring with her a stack of new records that she had bought in Mayo. She would place them upon our impressive radiogram in the dining room, and the sound of Irish lament for emigrants and exiles would ring out in that peaceful, Lancashire, semi-detached coalminer's house. We children would play around our mother's feet while she stood at the kitchen sink, washing up and looking out into the back garden, dreaming of her home in the West.

Before pop music ever took a hold of our young ears, the strains of old Ireland were well planted in our young hearts. To this day, my sister Tricia and I can knock out a fair duet of 'The Road by the River', a sad song of exile and lost love. How we love a good cry! 'With my little snubbed nose fastened up to the pane, sadly watching the rain as it makes little streams and the road by the river that flows through Raheen.'

My Mammy could not sing a note, and her attempts were always met with howls of laughter from us children. Mammy would then smile at us and say, 'Well, you sing it, then, for me.' I have been singing for my Mammy ever since. And song became the barometer by which my mother estimated the condition of my heart. If I was singing she knew I was happy. When song disappeared from my life, she knew dark days were upon me.

From my earliest days I would try to sing like the person on the record, and after one particular performance I looked up at my mother and asked, in my baby voice, 'Doadly shing, Mammy?'

Mammy replied, 'Yes, Brian, that was a lovely song.'

That phrase is my first recorded statement. It is a request for approval of my efforts, and it reminds me how important it is in life for us to give and receive affirmation to and from one another. My childhood request for approval became, ever afterwards, the comment on anything I ever did that was good. If I looked to my mother for approval, she would often smile and say, 'Yes, Brian, doadly shing.'

Irish melodies were played in our house whenever the gramophone was switched on. It was my Mammy's way of being in touch with the land that she loved, and with the home that she had never wanted to leave. She made her home in England and in Lancashire for nigh on 60 years, and ever grateful to England she remained to her dying day. But she missed Ireland, she missed Mayo, and she missed the town of Bangor Erris. But most of all she missed the Glen where she was born, and the people who were in it. That little spot, in the northwest corner of County Mayo, surrounded by gentle hills and bordering on the lovely lake of Carrowmore, was called Glencullen Lower.

To us children, Glencullen was the land of dreams, a place of summer joys, where we would play out the live long day with our cousins – eleven in Uncle Hugh's house and seven in Auntie Sarah's house – and mingling with dogs and hens and chickens and ducks, and cows even. It was a place where the smell of turf smoke at the fireside, and in the open air, spelled all that was magical and mysterious about this life of play, and we were the playboys and playgirls of the Western World. After coal dirt and coal dust, and the grime of an honest Lancashire town, it was another world to find ourselves waking up to a sunny morning in Glencullen, to a cooked breakfast waiting for us, to our cousins waiting for us to be ready to come and play, and to the turf fire of the night before, then covered with ashes, now burning brightly again to greet another day.

For my mother, it must have been a snatch of heavenly joy, a moment of bliss, to be there again, in her own place, her own land, visiting her own ageing mother, her brother, Hugh, and sister-in-law, my wonderful Auntie Annie.

For my father, whose own father had been a Mayo man from the Westport area, it was absolute heaven. Spending all year, as he did, underground hewing for coal, having spent his youth in the army and then fighting a war, it was a real joy for him to find himself now in the open air, with fields and mountain views, with Uncle Hugh for company and a glass of Guinness in the evening. My father could not and would not ask for more.

On many an evening Daddy and Hugh set off for Bangor and for the pint and the craic, that lovely Irish capacity for conversation and fun. Daddy loved life and always saw the funny side of it. He told me that one evening – or rather, one night – four of them were coming home from Bangor, after a session, on bicycles. It was a four-mile jaunt in the dark, around by the lake of Carrowmore and into the Glen. One fellow, who will remain anonymous, came to the 'Big Turn', as it is called, and decided to pedal straight on, and disappeared in the gloom over the edge of the road and into a soft landing in the bog. 'Are you all right?' his travelling companions asked him, and up from the darkness came the immortal reply, 'Arrah, this bicycle doesn't know me at all!'

One year, when the holiday was over, we climbed into the hired car for the journey back to Dublin and Dun Laoghaire, and to the ferry for Holyhead. This leaving was always a crying ceremony. Mammy would cry to be leaving her own mother and her own place. That would start Auntie Annie crying, as it would be another year before we came again. That would start us children off and before we knew it, it seemed as though the whole world was crying. Daddy would start up the engine and away we would go, looking out of the rear window of the car all the way to the 'Big Turn'. That was the spot where we first saw the homestead when we arrived, and the last place from which to view it as we left.

On this occasion, as we proceeded down along the lakeshore road through the townland of Cloontiakilla, we came upon a face that belonged to a cousin of my mother's, called Jack Cosgrove. On that quiet morning he was sitting on a grassy bank waiting for us to come along. Jack had been out the night before and had caught some fine fish for us. Two salmon, I think they were, and Jack was making a going-away present of them to my father.

We stopped the car and talked away as if there was no tomorrow, until finally Daddy had to tell him that we had a road before us. 'Well then,' said Jack, 'I won't be delaying ye. Let ye be driving and driving!'

That refrain has become a blessing in our house and family. Whenever we meet and wherever we go, we will often say to one another, in the blessing language of Jack Cosgrove, 'Let ye be driving and driving!'

Back home in Lancashire, and back at school, we would share our stories with our classmates. Where many of them had been away to Blackpool or Rhyl, and perhaps some had not been away at all, we had glorious tales to tell of magnificent vistas of blue and green, fields and skies, and of animals and rivers and fish. Of course, the story that really impressed our classmates was the one of our toilet arrangements. They were hugely impressed and hugely entertained by the fact that we went out to a cowshed, or out into a quiet corner of a field, to do our business. This was the real deal, as far as they were concerned. No holiday story could beat that!

Holidays over, my father went back to work down the pit, at Astley Green Colliery. We children went back to school at Sacred Heart School, Hindsford, and my mother went back to her life of washing, ironing, cooking, cleaning, shopping and taking care of us all. And she tended her garden, back and front and side, planting flowers at the front and vegetables in the back. And she said her prayers, and she took us to Mass, and she visited her sisters on Sundays in Manchester, or else they came to us. And she listened to the radio in the evenings while she knitted, and she played her records and thought of her home in the West, and saved up out of Daddy's hard-earned wage for us all to go again next year, when the summer time came round.

TWO

Exile

Mammy was born in 1916. All her life she kept her birthday in August, on the twentieth, but she also became aware that another date vied for the honour of being her date of entry into this world. When she died and her birth certificate was inspected, 5 September emerged as the official date. 'You were born on the day of the fair in Bangor,' her mother had told her, but there were two fairs at that time of year – one in August and one in September.

Her year of birth was a year of great violence in Ireland – the Easter Rising in Dublin, and the aftermath of the execution of the rebels, which then ignited the real fight for Irish freedom. Far away in the West, my mother grew up in a quiet glen. She knew nothing about the 'Troubles' or about the Civil War that raged through the land in her early years. But she heard the stories as she grew up about men on the run on Nephin Mountain, and about the ambush in Glenamoy.

She went to school in her native Glen, in a two-roomed building warmed by turf fires. I remember going to school there myself one summer, when we came to the West early. One class sat at the desks doing English, while another class stood round the wall doing religion. I was fascinated.

The school closed in 1970 and the building was later bought and converted into a holiday home. It is now the residence of one of the most appreciated public figures in Irish politics – his name is T. K. Whittaker and he was an economist. He planned the renewal of Irish economic life in the 1950s.

From the age of 10 until she was 12, Mammy was sent up the village to live with an old widow woman, to keep her company and to help around the house. This was not an unusual custom, apparently, but my Mammy did not like it one little bit, and she asked her own mother, 'Why do I have to live up there?'

At school, my Mammy excelled in her learning of the native Irish language, and her teacher made sure that she was in school when the inspector came round to examine the children in that subject. Mammy also loved poetry, and it was a custom in those days to teach children to memorise reams of poems. I know this first hand, for in my childhood days Mammy would sit me on her knee and recite episodes of the deeds of Brian Boru in never-ending verse.

But there is a lot about my mother's story that I do not know, and I put this down to the fact that I left home at the age of 11 and, from that time onwards, only came home for holidays from the priests' college. Ordinary times at home ended for me at that early age, and so the kind of stories I might have picked up about my mother's younger days, I never heard. However, I did hear stories about poteen – that fearsome Irish drink – and about how my mother was detailed by her mother not to come home from any dance without her brother, Hugh. Young men and drink can become fast friends, and the fallout from that we all know about.

My own childhood mirrored my mother's in that it was a blissfully happy time. Those years of infancy and junior schooling were years of complete happiness and, as such, they formed the secure and certain foundation of my whole life. I have no memory of sorrow connected to those years, only happy pictures in my head of a warm and contented home, a loving mother and a hard-working and kind father, two sisters, a brother and a collie dog. Add all that together and I was rich beyond counting. When, in later days, I went to seek help through counselling, Clare, my counsellor, assured me that I would be able to find happiness in my life again because of this rock-solid foundation of life that had been my early years at home.

An added ingredient in this early bliss was my little junior school, Sacred Heart, Hindsford. It was like a big family. The school, the church and the priests' house all sat on the same piece of ground, and while we were there, in class or in the playground, the church with its spire stood guard and sentinel over its little flock.

As I write these words, I am still in touch with my teacher from the days of Junior Three class, when I was 10 years old. His name is Ambrose Lavin. He later became headmaster of the school. His mother, from County Mayo, was a great Irish dancer, and she always insisted on my grandfather playing the fiddle when it came her time to step it out. Ambrose was the mainstay of the Hindsford story. As a young teacher, and later as headmaster, Ambrose saw several generations of children begin their lives under his watchful, caring eye. He has been a real shepherd to many children and families in that quiet corner of Lancashire.

The old school building is long knocked down, and the church, a beautiful little gem in its way, is locked up, and unused, its future uncertain.

My mother's happy life in the Glen is a story without stories for me. Her life in detail only really begins when, in 1935, aged 19, Ellen Rose Carey left the security and the peacefulness of her beloved home and her beloved mother and, travelling with her cousin, Kathleen McHale from the nearby village of Muingingaun, arrived in Manchester to join her sister, Bridget, and to find work in domestic service.

Exile, forced emigration, is a sad affair, even where people go on to make a success of it. Home is such a precious place, and to have to leave is a real sorrow. It has always happened in Ireland, and sadly it is still happening today. My mother loved her native place and would gladly have stayed there if there had been a life for her to live in that lovely country. Such was not the case, and across the sea she had to go.

I know what exile is like, for I, too, felt that I had to leave home, and at an even earlier age than my mother had. I was 11 when the Church encouraged me away to the seminary.

Did I go of my own free will? There is no easy 'yes' or 'no' answer to this question. Did I go because my mother made me go? No. I went because the Church, in the shape of a friendly priest, came and suggested to me that if I was interested in a vocation in the priesthood, then going to a junior college was what I should do. At the age of 11, being all good will and good intentions, and wanting to respond to a good thing that was being proposed, I said, 'yes', I would go.

The cost was to prove extremely high to me personally and to my family over the years, in terms of sadness, frustration, loneliness and simple unhappiness. And this only increased as the years went by. But we say 'yes' and we try to live up to 'yes'; we are encouraged to persevere, and we are praised on all sides for the great thing that we are doing.

Then some powerful messages taken from Scripture start to ring in our ears. 'Once the hand is laid on the plough, no one who looks back is fit for the kingdom of God' (Luke 9:62). How often did I hear that quote used as a reinforcement to young men to stay the course and to become priests?

'What about you, do you want to go away too?' (John 6:67). The burning question that was put by Jesus to Peter was also put to us aspiring students to keep us on that road of self-dedication.

My senior college was geared to keeping its students and seeing them through to priesthood. It was not geared or set up to weed out or help students 'discern' a different way of life. Leaving senior college was still regarded as a failure, and those who left were considered to be 'failed priests'. I even remember students in theology discussing, in front of us junior students, who were still only in philosophy, whether it was a mortal sin to leave the Order after one had committed oneself to final vows. Such was the narrow, hothouse world of seminary.

Away from other influences, away from other, ordinary people with other ways of looking at life, we, as young men, were stuck out there in the middle of nowhere (also known as Shropshire), being exclusively programmed. I hated it then, and I am sad at the very thought of it now. And I stayed!

An outsider might reasonably ask the obvious question: 'Why did you not leave? You were clearly unhappy. Why did you stay?'

There are a number of ways in which I try to answer this, a number of ways in which I try to understand it myself. The deepest reason that I can see now is that I had no experience of being in charge of myself. By this time, after all the years in junior college and then in senior college, I had lived in obedience, doing as I was told. I had no experience of life in the world. I had not even developed opinions of my own. I was not a self-starter any more. I was an obedient responder to religious direction. I felt as if I had handed myself over to the Order to programme me and prepare me for the great work of being a priest. Brian had, in fact, disappeared without trace in this seminary system.

My friend, David, from my childhood days, told me straight, years later: 'I lost you in the Church,' he said, in his straightforward and direct way. I felt as though I had been hit in the face when he said it. It stunned me to hear it, and only later on did I become fully aware of how truly he had spoken.

The six years that I spent in Shropshire, quiet and beautiful county that it is, were among the most miserable of my life. From 1965 until 1971 I lived in that Queen Anne country house that is known now as Hawkstone Hall, and I died there. As a spiritual human being with any kind of intellectual life, or even basic human drive, I perished.

The day of my ordination was no joy to me, but simply a further part of the process that was being done to me before I was shipped out into priestly ministry. My sister Tricia cried as she knelt at the altar to receive the first blessing from the new priest. Not tears of happiness for me, but tears of sorrow for the brother who had been taken from her when she was just 10, and who now was lost to her in the Church for evermore.

During the late summer of 2012, shortly before my Maggie died, I sat down and wrote a poem for myself that finally nailed the experience of Hawkstone for me. I have lived with silent anger and frustration over this place of my incarceration. I have told myself to let it go. I have softened for myself the fierce criticism that I hold inside myself about this time and this part of my life. But in the late summer of 2012 I found the words, sparse and spare, to accurately state the absolute condemnation of those years, and the damage they did to me. For my own sake, if for nobody else's, I needed to say it as it here stands. I needed to nail it.

The Priest

I was never free.
From under the sheltering roof of my parents' house
I went to the Abbey
and into obedience to priests;
and obedience was the virtue, the style of life,
and I was very good at doing what I was asked.
I was a biddable boy.

I lived confined
in the grounds and high-walled buildings,
in the routines of the holy regiment.
And when, at last, at seventeen,
it ended,
I went straight into the holy house in Scotland.

That sweet, short summer of '64
seemed like a peek at life.
David and Tyldesley and the pictures:
We saw *A Hard Day's Night* . . . just what I was in for!

The holy house was silly, foolish and cruel,
keeping young men confined,
teaching them the weary ways of monasteries.
A happy home for piety, and nothing else.

Then the day of Vows, and solemn seriousness.
Renouncing a world we had never known
and plunging ourselves into a Shropshire wilderness
for years and years and years.

I died in Shropshire, never came to life.
Life was the boy at eleven, since when
slow strangulation had led to this
bleak Salopian plain.

No walls were needed here.
Here endless plain, unreachable horizon.
And within, religious rounds,
scholastic gibberish and food.

No world, no church, no other people here.
A deserted English mansion
bought by black-robed priests
before Winston won the prize.

Long drives led out . . . to nowhere.
Just minor roads off lesser minor roads,
and minor lives within, lived in the minor key.

Then Ordination Day, colour and bunting.
People coming to SEE ME – after all this time!
I chain-smoked with nervy panic,
gave my glasses to Mum
and lay down to be anointed priest.

Tricia cried. For joy? No. For loss.

The Winston that I mention in the poem refers to the Churchill of that name who, after the First World War, was looking to buy a place in the country and who had his eye on Hawkstone, until the Redemptorist Order stepped in and bought the house and immediate grounds to be their seminary. It would be a place for training young men to the priesthood, miles away from anywhere, out in the middle of farmers' fields, away from any notion of human population and human contact. Had it been bought as an agricultural college, you could see the point! But, for the purpose of training priests? What can I say?!

The exile that I felt in those locked-away years, I tried to overcome in little ways. One day I tried to get home by hitchhiking while all the other students were on a coach tour in south Shropshire. I could not bring myself to join them, and instead, with a friend, tried to thumb my way home. What I did not realise at the time was that it was a bank holiday, and that there would be even less traffic on that minor road than there usually was. Not a thing came by to offer us the slightest chance of heading north. Even my escape plans came to nothing!

A more direct attempt at going home came when, in deep misery, I went to ask the priest in charge of students if I could go home to see my mother and father. He turned down my request, saying my mood was only a passing thing, and told me to go for a walk up the drive. He never again asked me how I was!

I have come to realise that all my behaviours over the years have been attempts to get back to the home I lost when I was 11. All my holidays as a priest, over the course of 25 years, I spent with my parents, going home to Ireland. I never wanted to take ordinary holidays of my own with any friends. Never once. I just wanted to go back to Mum and Dad and back to Ireland, to the land of my childhood joys. I was, in fact, still the little boy who really wanted, quite simply, to be with his own family.

I was the little boy who put himself, trustingly, into the hands of the Church to be formed, as they knew best, into being a priest. I yielded up any ambition for myself, as directed by the Order. I would have no will of my own. I was at the service of the Church. If you do this as a mature individual, as a grown person, the strength of your developed character will see to it that a healthy tension always prevails between the needs of the institution and your own personal drives and interests. The act of obedience is then the act of an adult. It is a freely given assent. But having entered the system so young, and being induced into the ways of obedience when still a child, I never knew, in those days, what it would be to possess my own personal power, my own will. My experience in seminary killed the drive for life that should live in us all. Obedience proved to be the disempowering of me in my youth.

Happily for me, the day dawned when, with the help of counselling, I stepped into my own shoes and my own authority, and found my way to Maggie, who was to become my wife. On that day I found my true home, the home of my adult self at last, and my long exile was over.

THREE

Domestic service

My Mammy's exile began with a job in a house in south Manchester as a domestic servant. She was 19 years old. It was a big house where the people took in lodgers, and so Mammy's duties involved cleaning all the rooms and making fires in the rooms, as well as washing and general housework. She started work in the early morning, after rising at 5.30am, and her day would last well into the evening.

At the close of the day she could be found sitting in the kitchen waiting until the mistress of the house decided that she did not need her any more and gave her permission to go to her own room and to bed. She had a half-day off on Wednesdays, when she would go to visit her sisters, and the mistress always checked that she went to Mass on Sunday mornings. That was Mammy's life for a few years until war broke out. Then life changed completely.

With the war came work at the Metro-Vickers factory where they made munitions, and now Mammy was amongst lots of other women at work. She made friends and went to Irish dances. She fell in love with a man she met at a dance, only to discover eventually that he was already married. It left her broken-hearted.

It was during these early years that her big sister decided to change their Irish-sounding names, so that they would fit in with the local scene more easily. Bridget renamed herself 'Bea', and my Mammy she renamed

'Eileen'. Ellen no more! 'And did you accept this change without complaint?' I asked Mammy one day.

'Yes,' she smiled back at me. The quiet sister was obedient to the older one. I was amazed. Your personal name is so precious that it is not an easy change to make, I would say. But the quiet Irish girl just did as she was bid. Her son would do the same many a time in later years!

These years of service and of hard work every day were to characterise my mother's entire life. From life and work on a farm in the west of Ireland to domestic service in Manchester to munitions work throughout the war years. These hard years would be followed by the domestic life and work of a young mother of four children. Then a return to the workplace, when my father's health broke down – work that would see her become a nurse and a matron of an old people's home.

Looking back at the story of her working career, it makes impressive reading but, as with every human life, living the story as it happens is a tale of struggle and of slowly emerging confidence. For example, when my father's health broke down and Mammy had to go to work to bring money into the house, her first thought was to go back into domestic service. After all, that was the only peacetime work she had ever known. But it did not take long for her to be out and about in the world for her to realise that she was capable of so much more.

A local hospital was recruiting auxiliary nurses and Mammy went there, to Astley Hospital, and so began her career of working with and tending to elderly people. She learned about medicines and drugs and did the hard work of lifting, turning and helping people to wash and dress. She was in her early forties by this time. She loved her work and spoke fondly of the people she met there, both fellow nursing staff and dear patients. One old man with whom she had wonderful conversations was called Cedric, and Mammy often spoke of him at the time and long after his death.

By the time I had completed my studies for the priesthood, Mammy had left that hospital and had started to work as a deputy matron in an old people's home in Leigh. The woman that I knew to be such a capable mother was now proving herself to be a very capable social worker, with excellent skills in being with others and caring for them.

I had been a stranger in my own family since the age of 11. Once you leave home and spend the greater part of your days elsewhere, you become a visitor and a stranger in your own home. Mammy did not like to hear me say this when I mentioned it years later. Her love and embrace for me never changed. But for me, the leaver, it was so.

As I have already mentioned, I think that all the years that followed my ordination to priesthood were years of trying to claw back the home life that I had missed. I spent all my free days, all my holiday time, in the company of my mother and father. It was during those years, after the age of 24, that I began to know my mother and father again in a personal way. Just think about it. From the age of 11 until 17 I was not at home except for holidays. During the years of senior seminary I did not get home at all. My parents had to come into deepest Shropshire for four days in the summer to visit me. That was hard for my dad. He found himself without a pub or a betting shop!

My mother's skills for life and for organisation were wonderfully expressed when it came time for me to be ordained priest. After all the 'holy bits' at college, we came home on buses that my mum had arranged, to the local Catholic parish hall where an evening reception of food and a bar were waiting for us. Mum had also booked a very good band to play. I forget their name now, but I heard them play on Radio 2 shortly after their gig at my ordination, so they were good!

I had nothing to do with all this arranging, being stuck out in the wilds of Shropshire. My mother did it all. A few years later I found myself organising parish dances in London, and it was then that I fully appreciated exactly how well my mother had done in putting the party together for me.

After being deputy matron for some years, Mammy applied for her own home to run, and was appointed as matron of a 40-bed home in Hindley, near Wigan. This was to be the pinnacle of her career. She was well respected by all, and her confidence was at its highest. Trainees were sent to her because of her great common sense in dealing with life as it occurs.

One day, when Mammy was about to show some official visitors around the home, an old lady in the lounge became quite agitated. Mammy discovered that the lady wanted to dance and so, pardoning her guests for a moment, Mammy took the lady's hands and they danced around the room. The old lady became calm and contented and went back to her seat quite happily, and Mammy continued with the tour.

When her working days were over, Mammy bought a bungalow for her retirement years. It was back in the town where my father had been born, and the two of them settled into that lovely little house together. Mammy, being still fit and energetic, shopped, cooked, cleaned and tended her garden with flowers, shrubs and vegetables, while my dad studied the form, enjoyed his tea and settled down to watch the racing on Channel 4. A fair division of labour!

My father's health was broken and, after some years of little jobs, and after his own personal struggle to accept the realities of his condition, he had settled to the life he could manage, and rejoiced in the wonderful woman who was his wife and life partner.

In that little bungalow, Mammy sat at an open counter that joined the kitchen to the living room. From that vantage point she could see everything in the main room while also being in position whenever a fresh brew of tea was called for. It also kept her out of the cigarette smoke that came with my dear old dad. This central position in the house was dubbed 'Houston Control' by my brother Michael, and was well named.

I think my mother struggled a little to accept the day of her retirement. It is always a big change in life, and you wonder what you will do next, now that the familiar routine and the reins of power are gone. But if she did struggle, it did not stop her life or activity at all. Mammy would often speak to me about 'Work – that blessed panacea!' So often, when we are down, we find that work and occupation ease the mind, taking our attention away from our worries, and filling our days with something good to do.

Those retirement days in the bungalow together would only last three years before my father died. It was a hard time for my mother after that. She was to spend another six years in that little house by herself, and she occasionally told me of the tears that she shed when she was on her own. At the time of Daddy's death, she did not cry much at all. She felt she needed to be strong for all her children. Only afterwards, when the world had gone back to work and to normal, everyday things, did she find her tears flowing. And two years later, at the funeral of Uncle Johnny, my father's brother, she found herself crying tears for Daddy that had remained unshed two years before.

It is the little things that we find ourselves remembering. Mum had to tell Dad that he needed to go into hospital. She could no longer manage him herself. The doctor had told her so. But Mum knew that Dad wanted to stay at home and to die in his own house. When she told him he would have to leave that little happy bungalow, she said, 'I saw him sitting on the settee, with his handkerchief in his hand to wipe his eye, and he looked up at the picture of Our Lady on the mantelpiece and he slowly shook his head.' It was that quiet acceptance by my father, and the pang of pain in my mother's heart because she could not do for him what he so dearly wished, that always stayed with her. She told me that story a few times.

In their latter days together, my dad would say to my mum, 'Oh Eileen, you'll outlive me by years!' And he was right. My mother lived for 22 years following my father's death. Born in the same year, 1916, my father was 71 when ill health took him. Mammy lived to be 94 before simple old age took her from us. They lie buried in different places, in different graves. Daddy is buried in his home town of Tyldesley. Mammy is buried in her home country and her home county of Mayo. They ended their lives where they had begun them, but oh, what a great circle of life they both lived!

Domestic service is a name we give to a particular kind of work at a particular time in the history of our society. It was hard, it was poorly paid, it meant long hours, and it was very often drudgery. But from those unpromising beginnings, my Mammy made her life into a life of sublime service, first to her children and family, then to the elderly people in her care, always to her beloved husband, and finally to the greater family that gathered around her in the final chapter of her life back in the West of Ireland. In 1994, at the grand old age of 78, Mammy sold up her bungalow and returned to the land of her birth, taking up residence in a granny flat attached to the lovely house that my sister Tricia had settled into, just below the town of Westport, County Mayo.

Mammy was to live there for 16 years, until her death in October 2010. For most of that time she lived a fairly vigorous life, walking the mile into town, going to Mass, doing her shopping and having a coffee before walking back home. She kept a part of the garden that was hers to tend. She made herself a proper cooked meal every day. Now in these final years, she had her two daughters living nearby, two grandsons and many visitors, including myself and my brother.

If the long road of her life seemed to be quietly coming to a close, such was not the case. At the age of 83, she was informed by her eldest son, for so long a priest, that he was leaving the priesthood and that there was a girl on the scene and a child, a boy of seven, a grandson she had never known about. Quite a shock for an old lady to take.

On the night that I phoned to tell her this news, I forewarned Tricia, who stayed with her and talked with her that evening. It was a very upsetting night, my sister tells me. Letters and phone calls followed, and a few months later I came over in person to see Mum and to explain more fully my story.

These situations are not so much about explaining things as they are about helping people to absorb the new reality and to cope with it. Once I knew my own mind fully and calmly, I knew I would be able to explain things to anybody, and most especially to my mum. It is when we are uncertain that agitation affects our soul and makes us unready to deal with life's issues. But I was sure. I knew my own mind, and I had never felt as assured about anything in my life.

A short while later, my friend, Ed Hone, a priest in the Redemptorists, also paid a visit to my mum. He was able to tell her the story from his own experience of living beside me, and that was a great help to her. 'I knew he was unhappy,' she told Ed, 'but I did not realise that he was so unhappy.'

The following springtime I came over to see Mum with Maggie and with my son, Michael. The two women who meant most to me in life met for the first time, and it was a gentle meeting. My Mammy could see with her own eyes that I was a completely happy man, and that was all she had ever wanted. Over the following years Mum and Maggie became the best of friends, happy and easy and loving in each other's company, Michael got himself another grandmother, and Mum another grandson.

The domestic circle of life was now complete. All was safely gathered in, and when Mammy died, we all gathered around her and prayed her into the loving arms of God.

FOUR

Life in a Lancashire town

Tyldesley is a Lancashire town par excellence, as the locals might say. It is a product of the industrial revolution, or at least it was in the 1940s and 50s. There were seven coalmines in action 'in the days when I were a lad', a cotton mill by the name of Caleb Wright, and another factory owned by Ward and Goldstone. Many of the streets were cobbled, and many of the locals wore clogs on their feet, including some of the children who went to school with me. The local 'lingo' was a bit special too, and people from only a few miles away from Tyldesley could struggle to fathom the vernacular and the dialect.

Into this Lancashire town came Eileen Carey as a young wife and mother. She came from Manchester with her husband, Michael Fahy, a native of Tyldesley, and newly discharged from the army after the war. In her arms was a three-month-old baby, my good self. We stayed for the first year or so with my father's brother, Uncle Tommy and Auntie Lily; we were given a warm welcome and every kindness in that house.

My dad went back down the pit where he had first started work as a 14-year-old, and we moved into our own newly built council house in September 1948, just after my sister Tricia was born. In our new home two more children came along – Sheila in 1952 and Michael Gerard in 1954. As we children grew up we came to realise many things about our environment and about ourselves.

We came to realise that we were slightly different from real Tyldesley people, in that we were half Tyldesley and half Irish. That is still my definition of myself. I feel English to the extent of being a Tyldesley boy, and a citizen of Lancashire. Of these things I am very proud, although my Englishness does not extend beyond these parameters. The rest of me feels hugely Irish, but in that special sense of belonging to one of the largest tribes on earth, the Irish diaspora.

From our earliest years we went away to Ireland every summer, and so, from those first years, we came to know that there was a world beyond Tyldesley, and a very different world at that. One world was all chimneys and coal dust and Lancashire accents, hard work and cobbled streets, and the other world, always visited during summer months, was a green and pleasant land, and it wasn't England. It was the Ireland of green fields and brown bogs, of mountains and lakes, of trout rivers, and of never-ending horizons.

For my mother, coming to Tyldesley must have been a huge shock. What she had known was Ireland West, then Manchester city suburbs and the buzz of wartime. Now, all of a sudden, when her stranger husband returned after two years of war following their wedding day, and they were getting used to one another again, she found herself for the first time in a town and a culture that she had never known. Believe me, Tyldesley was a very different kettle of fish from big city Manchester – in every way!

Learning the local language was a challenge in itself for a quiet Irish girl. When Mammy went to the shop to buy bread, she listened very carefully to the lady in front of her, to see what she would say. 'Two big 'uns and a rarnd 'un,' were the words that flowed out of that lady's mouth. Mammy's introduction to local dialect. It really was a world of its own, Tyldesley.

One of the local pubs was officially called 'The Welcome Traveller', on Elliott Street. But because the landlord, who, I presume, must have borne the Christian name of Robert, had a squint in his eye, the pub was always and affectionately known as 'Skenning Bob's'. 'Ah'll sitthee in Skenning Bob's toneet,' would be a common hail and farewell on the streets of Bongs. Oh yes, 'Bongs' was the nickname for the town, as it was built on a bank, on rising ground.

We lived on a new estate, 'up Shakerley' as the locals would say, and in those early days it was always referred to as 'up Wimpeys'. The Wimpey firm of builders had constructed the new estate immediately after the war, and it was built out in the fields on the north side of the town. It meant that we did not grow up in those cobbled streets of old Tyldesley, as my father had done, but in the open places of this new area, very close to a farm, to open country. Further up the fields there was a railway line, carrying trains from Manchester Victoria to exotic destinations such as Wigan and Southport.

The people of Tyldesley were a friendly sort. We were all working class, and worked in the pits, the mill or the factory, mostly. But our origins were quite diverse. I learned in later years that the village of Tyldesley became a town when the mines were sunk, and workers came from Cornwall and from Wales to find work there. These people formed the non-conformist tradition of chapels that sprung up around the town. A chapel on Tyldesley's main square, known as Top Chapel, was built for the

Lady Huntingdon's Connection, the Calvinistic branch of
the Methodist Church. Added to this mix were the Irish
farm labourers who came out of the Cheshire farms to
find employment in the darkness of the mines and in the
depths of the earth.

Like any group of outsiders, the Irish formed their own
community in an area called Squires Lane, and it was
there that my grandfather settled when he met a local girl
and made Tyldesley his home. He had been heading for
America and for the city of Chicago, where his sisters had
emigrated, but meeting Maggie Trumble set him on
another road. 'I had the two shoes bought for going to
America,' he would say, 'when I met this colleen.'

My grandfather, Michael Fahy, was a lovely old man.
Short build and stocky, waistcoat and moustache, and
musical. He played the fiddle and the flute in his young
days, and was much called upon whenever dances were
arranged in Westport, Newport and Lahardaun, in the
Mayo days of his youth. But poverty and the need for
work brought the young man over to Cheshire to work
the farms with his own father, and to sleep in barns at the
end of the day. The move to Tyldesley and to the mines
followed, and meeting my grandmother, Maggie Trumble,
did the rest.

I have one particular memory of my grandfather,
which is very precious to me. I was 15 years old and
home from boarding school for Christmas, and it was
night time and very cold, with snow on the ground. My
mother and father happened to be out, and we four
children were at home. My grandfather lived next door to
us by that time. Suddenly there was a knock on the door
and a neighbour told me urgently that my granddad was

halfway down the street, clad only in his nightshirt. He had gone out to the outside toilet, to save himself climbing the stairs, and being almost blind, he had missed the door on returning to the house. With every step he took he was going further away from his home. I ran down the road and put my arms gently about his shoulders – Granddad was literally shivering – and told him who I was. Turning him round, I guided him slowly back to his own home and hearth. He sat down again by his fireside and I made him a big mug of tea. He was so grateful.

The house he was in was poor, and there were bare boards showing in the living room. I felt so sad for him, at the end of his life to be sat on his own, a widower now of some five years. I have often recalled the incident, and thought of my grandfather's long and hard-working life, and of the little cottage back in Mayo that I have visited and from which my grandfather set out into the wide world. And I have felt the happiness of the night that I rescued my grandfather from the cold.

It is a wonderful thing to do kindnesses for people, and to care sincerely for them. I was not at home enough to do more for my granddad, being away in junior seminary, but that occasion fell to me, and I still cherish the moment today, 50 years later.

As a teenager I used to go to the Catholic club in Hindsford, a place that was commonly referred to as 'Paddy's Hump'. It was an old, large house, perched on rising ground, donated by a local businessman to the Irish community. There was a bowling green out front, and inside a full-sized snooker table, and various rooms. My dad was secretary there for a while, and in the mornings at eleven o'clock I used to go there and have a game of snooker. I always remember leaning down to take a shot – a red into the far corner – and as I steadied myself and got my eye in, I realised that I was looking directly into the eyes of Pope Pius X. There was a picture of this holy gentleman on the far wall, and he had now come into my line of fire. You cannot get any more 'Catholic club' than that! Many a time my granddad would be sitting in a side room enjoying a pint of 'mixed' – half bitter and half mild.

A very dramatic incident that I recall from those early years centres on my sister Tricia. She was always getting into scrapes, but this one was dangerous. One morning she was playing in our next-door neighbour's house with a girl called Dorothy. Dorothy's mum was out at the shops, and when she returned she thought there was a funny smell in her kitchen. She called over to my mum who went straight across and said at once, 'It's gas!' They went further inside the house and found the two girls unconscious in the dining room. Leaking gas had overcome them. They were carried outside and laid on the grass, and the doctor was called. Dorothy came round quickly, but Tricia did not seem to be responding.

At this point, standing there looking at my prone sister, I began to feel desperate. I turned on my heel and ran inside my own house, into the dining room, and knelt down in front of an armchair. There was a cushion on the chair and I buried my head as hard as I could into the cushion and prayed to God to save my sister. I kept pushing my head as hard as I could into that cushion. It was the most insistent prayer I have ever prayed. It was a physical entreaty. My sister came round.

There is an echo of that experience in the way my Maggie died. On that last morning, as the cerebral tumour was about to take her life away, Maggie stirred in bed and buried her head into the middle of my back, between my shoulder blades. Being asleep, I only half woke and called her name to stop. I was too sleepy to realise what was happening. Only later, only afterwards when everything was over, did I become aware of what had really taken place in that early morning hour.

Maggie was pushing her head into me, perhaps to try and relieve the pain, but also and clearly trying to reach me in her semi-conscious state. I see everything in that moment and in that gesture. She was reaching out for help, trying to reach me, because we belonged together and we loved each other so much.

Only on two occasions in my life have I experienced this act of pushing ferociously hard with one's head: the day my sister nearly died and the day when my Maggie did die. Those moments are forever joined in my memory now.

In the summer of 1960, when I was 13, a group of us became very enthusiastic about athletics. It would have been during the summer of the Rome Olympics. We went over to a sports ground in a village called 'Gin Pit' and ran round the track like good athletes. It was glorious summer weather. Some of the lads who did not know me very well started to ask me what this funny college was like; one lad in particular asked me a question that made me roar with laughter at the time, and ever since. In a broad Tyldesley accent he inquired, 'Ee, Briun, dost tha 'av to 'av thi 'air shaved off when tha goes t't monkery?'

I hope you can read that! At the time I had a full head of hair, very much like Elvis Presley. Sadly, now, it has all gone with the wind! And the boy's question proved accurate, for when I went to the monastery at 17, the priest there made me have three haircuts in one day, to reduce my locks to a severe crew cut. The idea behind this brutality was to remove all traces of pride from our minds.

Coming home from our athletic endeavours on the running track, my friend David and I used to go into a temperance bar where we were served 'Long Toms'. These were long glasses of shandy – beer and lemonade – and sitting there drinking them we felt like grown men on the beer. At 15, this is a very important sensation and marks the beginning of growing up and of changing from child to adult.

It was at this point in my life that my experiences of living in this ordinary world and this happy Lancashire town were ended. The 'monkery' that my friend referred to took me away from ordinary life, and in doing so did me no favours whatsoever.

Looking back now on those teenage years, I see very clearly the wrong that was done by the Church in encouraging boys of such tender years to say goodbye to home and family, to come away from friends and home environment, to leave the natural surroundings and routines of ordinary life – school, sport, pals, girls, local life, cinema, even parish life; in fact, every little thing that makes up a normal growing up – and placing those young boys in the narrow confines of a school, with strict rules and regulations, a day-long discipline, no contact with outsiders, and the unspoken presumption that you stay well clear of girls!

The enormity of the injustice stands out clearly to me today. At the time, I entrusted myself to a system and to the people who ran it, because they were older than me, and they were in the Church, and that was how things were done, and the Church was a holy place.

I lost all the natural contacts and ties at home that would have been part and parcel of any child's growing up. It began a pattern of repression in me that eventually became my mode of survival in the Church. I suppressed all my natural feelings and I was not conscious of the harm it might do to me. The Lancashire/Irish boy disappeared inside and the Latin-learning, Greek-excelling, bright lad was on the conveyor belt to Roman Catholic priesthood in a Religious Order.

FIVE

The sixties

I left Tyldesley behind me for the final time in the summer of 1964. The Beatles were all the rage. I went to see *A Hard Day's Night* with my friend David, and shortly after that I boarded a steam train in Manchester and went north to Scotland and to the 'novitiate', a spiritual training year. I arrived in Perth and was ferried up the hill to the monastery (or 'monkery'!) on Kinnoull Hill. It would be there, in that holy place, that I would one day, 27 years later, meet Maggie and find my own salvation.

It is strange the little things you notice as you go along, things that return to you in later days as significant moments. On that journey to Scotland, a land I had never before visited, I remember the train pulling into Stirling station. As the carriage came to a stop, I looked out the window and saw a little semi-circular kiosk on the platform. It was a newspaper stall that was selling papers, magazines and sweets. It looked so compact and cosy, it gave me a feeling of homeliness just to see it. Many years later that place, Stirling, the sight of that homely vision, became and remains my home.

I remember the train pulling slowly out of Stirling that day, and meandering through the little village of Bridge of Allan. What a lovely name, I thought to myself as we went by. It is the only part of that long journey that I can recall. I travelled from Manchester, via Preston and Carlisle, up to Perth. But I just remember calling into Stirling and that slow passage through the Bridge of Allan. Take a good look, Brian, and remember.

Going into the novitiate was called 'leaving the world'. And that is exactly what I did, exactly what happened to me, and it was the worst thing that I could possibly have done. But I did not know that at the time. How could I, in any real sense, leave a world that I had not yet even begun to discover?!

This 'holy' year got off to a very dramatic start. I had sent my suitcase on ahead by British Rail, but I did not insure it, and sure enough, the case never arrived. All my clothes were in it, so when I left the world behind, I did so absolutely! On one of our first long walks in the countryside, a fellow novice found a shoe and said to himself, 'If I can find the other, then Brian can have another pair for himself.' However, when he did find the other shoe, it was unfortunately attached to a body. A poor man had thrown himself off the hill and we had found him.

A week later, on another long walk, this time near the town of Crieff, we came back into the main street. As we walked along, a dark limousine came crawling by. It stopped for a moment and as I looked at the occupants, I found myself looking into the faces of Ringo Starr and George Harrison. The Beatles were on tour in Scotland and were making their way to the Caird Hall in Dundee. My brush with fame! They were all smart suits and mop tops and screaming girls. I was all black suit and crew cut and 'Hail Marys'!

In the year of 1964 I ought to have been going to university. I ought to have been discovering girls and learning how to grow up, but instead I was programmed into a religious routine of prayer and pious lectures, work and long walks in the country, and no contact of any kind with other human beings. No newspapers, no radio, no television, no outside connection at all.

The one pop record that was in the building and which we played ad nauseam was Little Eva singing 'The Loco-Motion'! 'Everybody's doing the Loco-Motion', she sang, but we weren't![4] And the only television we were allowed to see occurred in January 1965 when we watched the state funeral of Winston Churchill.

When the holy year was over, we took vows to live lives of poverty, chastity and obedience. These vows were temporary, of three years duration, after which we would take final vows for life. Yet even as we took these temporary vows we were solemnly instructed that our intention ought to be that we were taking them for life. Programmed and indoctrinated, urged and encouraged – whatever way you describe it, it was very much an inducing of young men into a narrow world.

Vows taken, we were transported down to the wilds of Shropshire, to Hawkstone Hall, which, as I have indicated, was to become my religious prison for the next six years.

If you see it today, indeed if you see it any day, Hawkstone is a grand and a beautiful place, a Queen Anne country house, built for the Hill family of Shropshire. But in the days when I lived there, it was a remote institution, visited by no one, an isolated and separated place. It was off the beaten path, off the map, off the planet! Around 40 students were housed there with about a dozen teaching staff and house brothers.

I arrived one cold and misty night in late October 1965. All the students came down from the isolation of their rooms to welcome the seven new boys, but it felt to me

---

4. Gerry Goffin, Carole King, 'The Loco-motion' (1962).

more like we were being gawped at, something new in an otherwise sombre sameness. After only a few days I wrote home to my mother to say how unhappy I was, and she replied to say that if I was really unhappy then I should come home. But faced with such a prospect, and having only just taken vows, it suddenly began to feel immature not to persevere through the early hardships, so I struggled on.

I find myself reluctant to speak very much about these years. It would all be very negative and would not serve any purpose now. 1965 to 1971 were the years of my incarceration, years when a great deal was going on in the world. The swinging sixties, the Vietnam War, the political grimness of the UK, the student rebellions of 1968: all these things and many more were happening, but away in the wilds of Shropshire you would not have known it.

We literally saw nobody apart from the resident community of our own selves. I protested about this as I became a more senior student. I called meetings to try and put over the point that a remote college in the middle of nowhere is not the place in which to train young men for anything, and certainly not a helpful place in which to train people for priesthood. I still have the notes I prepared for that meeting 40 years ago. My main argument was based on the evil of isolation. My notes read:

Isolation – geographical, social, educational, pastoral. Total divorce of priestly education from the mainstream of national education. A clerical ghetto – in fact a Redemptorist ghetto within the clerical ghetto. How can you form a priest in a rural backwater, away from the influence of people and human situations?

I was a voice crying in the wilderness, but I did not have the power, clout or personality of John the Baptist with which to drive home my protest.

I was also a child, living in total obedience to my superiors, and I had been like that since the age of 11. My mind and my intellect had developed, but neither my emotions nor my character had ever been able to develop. I had never known the cut and thrust of student life that an ordinary education would have given me. Only on the football field did my natural self find any expression.

On a football field, I have never felt anything but the exhilaration of freedom and self-confidence. At college, the few games we played against outsiders were usually against other seminary teams, and my abiding memory of 'glory' – that quality of life that meant so much to the Tottenham player, Danny Blanchflower – came when we made the trip to Oscott College in Birmingham and played them off the park . . . for 15 minutes!

I was the captain of the side in those days, and I had called a meeting to talk tactics a few days before the game. 'The man on the ball is not the most important player at that moment,' I told them. 'It is the other players and the options that they create for the man on the ball that count.' This was divine revelation to some of my listeners, but they liked what I said and they absorbed it. I got the team playing 'triangles of passing and movement', creating multiple options for the man on the ball.

At half time in the match, and with our side leading 3–1, my old history teacher from junior college, Father Parker, who was watching from the touchline, came up to me and said, 'In all my years I have never seen a Hawkstone team play such great football.' I was pleased and started to go round the group urging more of the same. One of the players turned round to me and told me to back off, and, as I am not an aggressive person, I did. Consequently, the second half was a shambles as the team forgot all the good things they had done in the first half and, finding themselves under pressure from determined opponents, they resorted to kick and rush. We survived to win the game 3–2. I was so annoyed! I should have put that player in his place!

When I was ordained priest in August 1970, I was really a baby-priest. That is what the system had produced. There are no two ways about it. I remember a time in London, years later, when I was assisting one of my old priest teachers, then a parish priest out near Wembley. We were reminiscing about Hawkstone, and he said to me about his own life journey, 'I went into the seminary a boy of 17 years, and I emerged from the seminary seven years later, still a boy of 17 years.'

Becoming a priest is a lifelong journey, and student days are important. It is not healthy to separate students from ordinary life. It is not healthy to keep students locked away from ordinary people and places. It is not healthy to impede students in the vital experience of growing up. It is not healthy to keep young men away from women. Our emotional lives, our sexual development and the experience of human relationships are vital issues at this stage in life, and to be kept corralled out in the countryside did nothing to promote or develop these vital energies.

Whenever we students gathered together for recreation, on occasions of celebration and feast days, the music would be turned on full blast and all together at the top of our voices we would sing the anthem of The Animals rock band.

> We gotta get out of this place,
> if it's the last thing we ever do.
> We gotta get out of this place.
> Girl there's a better life for me and you.[5]

It was unnatural to put us young men out there in the fields of Shropshire. The life force that was in me died out there. I wrote a piece in an exercise book back then, and I have kept it ever since. I have never shown it to anybody, but I think now is the time. I was about to leave Hawkstone to go to London as a curate in a parish beside Clapham Common. These are my final words about the six years I spent in Shropshire – the words I wrote at the desk in my little room in 1971:

> Subjection to a system, acquiescence in an unaccepted routine will dull and cloud the life in a person. The dullness of the years at Hawkstone, the absence of promise, of vision, of journey, of search, kills the life of the human spirit.
>
> Philosophy was dead, a dead enclosed system, cut off from life. Church History was the annals of dead men past. Sacred Art was irrelevant chatter on the beauties of the world. Dogma brought the promise of life but kept it out of reach. Morals with Jim challenged the mind but the environment choked it. Scripture did not exist. Canon Law belonged to the circus, but was tragi-comedy. Morals with Griff was sludge in slow motion.

---

5. Barry Mann, Cynthia Weil, 'We gotta get out of this place' (1965).

> I emerge from Hawkstone dripping with indifference, carried on by God and friends, with a great need to smash the encrusting sloth of six years in the wilderness.

The first person singular is missing from that opening paragraph, revealing how unable I was to say anything really personal about myself. But today the translation is simple: in Hawkstone I was sad, I was miserable and my spirit died.

My mother never knew these things. I never told her. She made an offering of her son to the Church, letting me go where I showed interest and where others led me. She prayed for her son every day of her life. She felt great honour and pride in the path that I was embarking upon, and in all her letters to me over the years – letters that I never kept – she always encouraged the goodness of my heart and shared pieces of advice and wisdom with me as they came along.

Did I become a priest because of my mother? No. Did I stay in the system because of my mother? No. At least I am not conscious of doing so, and I have no remembrance of my mother ever pushing me into anything. But the whole system pushed that way. Once you had shown an interest and become involved in the system, the system, like a powerfully running river, carried you along with great force out into the sea of priesthood. And everyone on the riverbank clapped and urged you on. That was the kind of atmosphere in which becoming a priest was conducted. And if you paddled your boat to the side and lifted yourself out of the river, people were not quite sure how to react.

The Church is a powerful reality and, when you are inside it, you can feel quite tiny if you start to think differently from the general stream of life within it. The relationship of the individual to the group is of vital importance, and the clashes that take place between organisation and individual are very necessary for the healthy operation of both parties. A real eye opener for me on this matter came when I was a student in Rome, in my mid-thirties, and studied sociology for the very first time. The forces of conformity in human life are quite frightening. We need 'awkward individuals' to keep us on the right track.

I believe Saint Benedict, in his 'Rule', instructs a community that if they have a house of complete harmony, with no dissenting voices or difficult characters in it, then they should send to a neighbouring monastery and recruit an awkward individual from there. A totally peaceful community is in great danger of becoming self-satisfied and of practising collusion.

I have found certain films to be most inspiring in this regard. *The Winslow Boy* is a classic tale of the power of the State almost crushing the individual, and it is in that film that we hear the great cry, 'You shall not side with the great against the powerless.' Another film on this theme is *The Verdict*, starring Paul Newman and James Mason. Church, society, political party, union, indeed any group, can become an overbearing bully in the life of an individual if a lively criticism is not flourishing.

The day I left Hawkstone, in July 1971, my mum and dad came to collect me for the summer holidays. Dad let me drive the car out of the seminary grounds, and I remember not looking back! Where did we go? Yes, off to the West of Ireland for our holiday. I was once again the little boy with his mum and dad going back to the land of happiness. It was as if Hawkstone had never happened. The real world lay outside at the far end of Hawkstone's long driveway. The real world was the place I had inhabited until the age of 11. Since then I had been an acquiescent party to a process of religious formation, which now let me out again, into the world, neatly dressed in a black suit and with a white collar.

Some years later, a conversation was reported to me. My old Greek teacher, Father Mythen, seeing me depart junior seminary en route to a life at Hawkstone, had expressed anxiety that 'Hawkstone might destroy his spirit.' It was with a rueful smile that I heard this comment, and sadly had to agree.

Not a happy chapter in my life. Not a happy chapter to write!

SIX

Adult years

Mum spent the sixties working as an auxiliary nurse. My dad's health was broken and he struggled to adapt and to adjust to smaller jobs while mum became the breadwinner. These years are all reported years to me; I was never there to see them. My sisters tell me of dad's dark days, when a sombre mood was on him, but he came through.

My sisters both trained to become teachers, and my little brother, Michael, seven years my junior, after following my example and entering a seminary – only this time a local one – made the decision at 18 to leave. He trained as a teacher and was to spend his whole working life in 'special education', dealing with teenagers from disturbed emotional backgrounds.

Mum and Dad gave us all a good start in life, by their love for us, by their care and hard work, by giving their all for their children. I remember one day meeting my brother for a pint in the Punch Bowl in Atherton. As we stood at the bar we looked over towards the door and saw our dad sitting there quietly with his pint, getting ready for the afternoon racing. He was looking back at his two sons with a smile on his face that spoke of his immense pride in his children. You never forget moments like that.

As my siblings grew into their own life journeys of work, careers, relationships, marriage and children, I felt like an adjunct in their lives, an added-on extra. They were always welcoming to me, each one of them, but I never felt as though I had a life in the same sense that they had a life. I was some sort of religious addition to other people's life stories. It sounds almost pathetic to say it, but it simply reflects the truth that I had not grown into the priesthood; I had not fully embraced it as a mature grown-up. Rather I just found myself in it as the end result of a formation programme, a quiet and obliging boy in clerical dress.

I now went wherever I was sent and carried out my priestly duties as I was expected to. Parish life in London. Parish missioner in Scotland. Back to the parish in London, then back to Scotland again. Was I happy in these roles? No. But happiness was not placed high on the agenda of life for a priest, according to my training. We were at the service of others, and sometimes life is hard, and those were the guidelines by which I tried to live my life. But with each passing year, it became gradually borne in on me that unhappiness was becoming my basic condition.

Then, a few years into priesthood, I fell in love. The episode ended in sorrow. I could not follow through on the love I felt, and I came away, but I never really got over it. I never fully recovered.

I went back into the priestly world and work, and for years afterwards I was emotionally crippled. My priest friend, Ed, named it well when he said of me that I had lived those years with low-level depression. The depression of my seminary years was now compacted with the depression of an unresolved love affair.

My father was very gentle with me during this struggle. I had gone home to my parents to try and face my issues, and my father came to me for a few minutes each day and gave me a thought for the day. He also took care of my mum who was not coping at all with the prospect of her priestly son about to leave and go off with a woman. I remember him saying to me, 'Brian, if you are unhappy in the life, then leave and I will help you to find a job. But if you are happy in the life, then do not leave it for a woman.'

Being in love tends to remove all other considerations from view, and I was in no position to calmly assess my life. I was not happy in the life, but it was the only life I knew. The issues in my heart and in my life story would need a great deal more unravelling than my father's advice could hope to resolve, but I never forgot it. In its brevity, it did capture a truth about the difference between identity and relationship: before you can fully relate to others you do need to discover who you are. You do need to have some sense of yourself. The strength of our human relationships finds its power precisely in our self-understanding and our healthy sense of ourselves.

Despite living with this low-level depression, I was able to function after a fashion, and I continued to be a parish missioner, travelling about the country, visiting homes and preaching in various places. Then, in the summer of 1982, Chris, a guy I had gone through the system with from my first year in junior college, came to me and urged me to go for a sabbatical somewhere. He could see how I was run down and going nowhere. He was all for suggesting California but I, being meek and unadventurous, with no real zest for life, opted to go to Rome and to live in our Redemptorist monastery, our central house of the Order, and to attend the college there.

You can see how timid I was, how unwilling to step outside the unhappy yet secure world I knew.

So in September 1982 I set off for Italy and a two-year study course in Moral Theology. I did very well in those studies, for I take immense pride in whatever intellectual pursuit I undertake. Those studies gave me, for the first time in my life, a sense of purpose and of achievement, after the insult of an educational life that I had experienced in Hawkstone.

The Redemptorist House in Rome, a truly international community, is situated on Via Merulana, just down the street from the great basilica of Santa Maria Maggiore. At breakfast time, as I sipped my coffee, ate my fresh bread and began to try out my Italian language on my new confreres, I could look out of the window and find myself gazing at the impressive mass of the Colosseum, hardly a stone's throw away.

Going into class in the great lecture hall, at first I was timid, and the notebook I took into lectures was hardly bigger than a postage stamp! But soon I began to feel I was going places, and the notebooks became A4 pads. I enjoyed the simple pleasures of Rome, the food and the 'vino', but I was also very aware that my ability simply to be happy was non-existent. The depression was a constant companion. Had I been truly happy and relaxed, my Italian would now be perfect, and my travel experiences of Italy would be deep and wide, but that did not happen. I was hamstrung. I was an emotional cripple, and my capacity for simple joy was very limited.

The two years in Rome, however, and the study that I did, gave me new energy, mental and intellectual energy, and this would stand me in good stead. Although my emotional life was a sad and secret business, known only to myself in any detail, my public life and my mental energy were functioning well again, much better than they had been before I went to Italy. For this I remain eternally grateful to the Eternal City, and to the people I met in Rome. The Accademia Alfonsiana, part of the Lateran University, did me proud and I will always be grateful to that institution.

At the end of my course of studies, I went to see the secretary of the college, a jolly and amiable French Canadian by the name of Roger Roy. He totted up all my marks from all the courses I had attended, from seminar work and from the dissertation that I had presented, and he said to me, 'There we are. *Magna cum laude.*' My heart sank. This was a second grade mark. I have always been top of the class in my studies, since the day I went to school. I was not accustomed to coming second and receiving lesser grades. Suddenly Roger said, 'Wait a minute. I've added that wrong.' He did the sums again, looked up at me and said, 'I thought so. *Summa cum laude.*' The highest mark. That's how I like it! Little did he know what torment I had just endured!

I came back to England, not, as I thought, to be a simple professor in the college in Canterbury, where our students now resided, but to be in charge of those same students, as rector of the house and in charge of their spiritual welfare as 'Prefect of students'. I also had to teach theology of the moral and pastoral kind, and teach a course on preaching. As well as this, as time went by, I was to be a part-time chaplain at Canterbury prison. This was in addition to a role as assistant to the provincial Superior of the Redemptorists in the UK. It was far too much. In the previous seminary system these various jobs would have been shared out among many priests, but with the reduction in manpower, multitasking was becoming the norm. Not a good idea! Not good for me, and not good for the students. I ought to have been hauled in front of the monopolies commission!

I was in Canterbury for six years, trying to do all these things – teacher, chaplain, student guardian and provincial assistant. The energy began to wane. The depression was always there somewhere. My fortieth birthday came during the middle of my time there, and I remember driving down to Dover and sitting on the cliff tops above the busy harbour, looking out to sea. It was that long kind of looking that says, 'I am lost.' This is my life, I thought, and I am not happy. I thought of my father and of how he had had no choice in his life about the things that had happened to him, especially losing his freedom for six years in a war. I likened my own six dark years in seminary to his six dark years in warfare, in order to try and help myself accept the incidental unhappiness of life. It did not make me feel any better.

Then one day I was asked to become a member of a group called *The Beginning Experience*, and some light began to dawn for me. *The Beginning Experience* is a programme of weekends – Friday evening to Sunday afternoon – where people gather who are 'stuck in their grief'. This might be the grief of being widowed, the grief of separation and divorce, or the grief over any kind of loss. Through a programme of talks, through shared and guided discussion, through quiet personal time and journal writing, and through shared prayer and Eucharist, the participants find themselves being freed from emotional paralysis, and light begins to come in where before only darkness reigned.

I went along as a participant first of all, and did my own grief work. During that weekend, I was challenged by two of the women who were leading the weekend. There were certain things that I needed to face up to, they told me, gently yet firmly. I had to face up to the depression inside myself and the reasons for it. I began to see a way into the light.

I remember coming back to Canterbury where one of the students saw the changed look on my face as I emerged from my car. 'What happened to you, then?' was his startled inquiry. There must have been a glint of brightness in my countenance. A chink of light had appeared.

Subsequent meetings, in which I was a part of the team, helped me to make further progress with my issues. I cannot speak too highly of this programme, or about all the lovely people that I met in the course of my short time with the group.

It was a short time, for the simple reason that in the summer of 1990, after the soccer festival of Italia '90, I was transferred from the student house and relieved of all my duties there. I was appointed to Scotland, to the house in Perth as a sort of house director of courses, the house where, 25 years before, I had set out on the journey into Redemptorist life and priesthood.

I felt that I was going nowhere. The mental energy that I had gained in Rome was wearing thin, and of course my emotional energy was flat. I had no great desire to do anything, so I told my superior, when I was asked for my views, that I had no ambitions of my own. It was not easy therefore for a superior to know what to do with me, or where to send me. As it was, I journeyed back to Perth. Little did I know, but the journey was about to become very interesting indeed.

SEVEN

Meeting Maggie

In Perth I found myself responsible for all the groups and guests who came to visit and to stay at the monastery. I had to prepare talks for these groups, and I had to be available to receive people individually who might come to me for confession or, more extensively, to talk over their worries and concerns. I was also the administrator of the house, and I found myself just as busy as I had been before. But I was more lonely.

On the day I arrived in Kinnoull, our monastery on the hill above the city of Perth, there was a letter waiting for me from my companion to priesthood, Chris. I opened the letter to find that Chris, who had been studying in Canada, had made the decision to leave the priesthood and religious life and, in fact, had just got married.

I sat on the bed in my room and felt completely abandoned, marooned. Chris and I had been together as students and friends since the age of 11, in 1958. We had come to this monastery together at the age of 17. We had gone through Hawkstone together and been ordained side by side. We had been appointed to London together and then to Perth together in our first years of priesthood. Our separation had only occurred in 1973, when Chris went to the publications house in Jane Austen's village of Chawton and I returned to Clapham Common once more. Now he was out in the wide world and here was I still going round in circles in religious life.

In those first months in Kinnoull, as I sat down to think and to write talks for visitors, I found myself writing about the human life journey and about the burden of the life story that we carry about with us every day. I can see now how very autobiographical those talks were, in their sources. I suddenly found people responding 'big time' to what I said, and many people wanted to talk to me as a result. Some people's cases were very heavy and were, in fact, beyond my ability to help. These people needed the help of a trained counsellor, which I was not. I gave them the space and the peace of the monastery, and I listened and reflected as best I could, but I also admitted that the real help they needed lay elsewhere.

Then, one evening in April 1991, the phone rang and a lovely Scottish voice began to talk to me. She told me her name was Margaret Corr, and asked whether it would be possible for her to come up to Kinnoull for a few days and talk to someone. No problem at all, I told her. The next day I met the lovely face that accompanied the lovely voice, and arranged times when we could meet. She was lovely through and through.

We had meetings over two days, and they were as rewarding to me as they were to Margaret. When we were done, Margaret asked me if she could have a hug. So we hugged. And we were both feeling that we wanted to see one another again.

So began the story of the rest of my life. Suddenly I was involved in the life of another person, and that person was involved in my life. It was a wonderful feeling.

As I was working in the house in Kinnoull, Margaret was working in a care home for the elderly along the River Tay, in a place called Leng, across from Dundee. Meeting Maggie and going out for days with her and for lovely coastal walks was truly refreshing, and I came alive. I was overjoyed to have found this beautiful girl, and she was so happy to be with me.

Our short, sweet summer lasted from April until October 1991. Then, with Margaret expecting a baby and me required to leave my position and to go elsewhere to 'think things through', we had to say goodbye to one another. The rest of the story, from my point of view, is told more fully in an earlier book, *Finding Maggie*.[6] Seven years of struggle involving counselling, the achievement of self-authority in my own life, wandering in a no-man's-land of indecision, and then the day of enlightenment, when everything fell into place and all became crystal clear.

But for Margaret and from her point of view, what a story of faithful and persevering love it is! She carried her baby and moved back to Stirling. She gave birth to a lovely boy, Michael, who is now 20 years of age. She went to train in Dundee College and became a qualified social worker. Her own mum looked after Michael and formed a powerful bond with her grandson. Margaret obtained a position in Clackmannan council social work office and flourished in her work.

She listened to my phone calls and received my letters and replied to them. She arranged caravan holidays for the three of us for three summers around the Moray Firth. She let me visit and she let me go again, until it became clear that Michael was getting to an age when it would be confusing for him. After one particular visit to her flat, when I stayed for two or three days, I said goodbye, but Michael blocked the door and would not let me go. It was heartbreaking, and when I finally left, I was in tears going

---

6. *Finding Maggie* (Kevin Mayhew, 2013).

down the spiral stairway. But it was harder still, I now realise, for the ones who were left behind.

The seven years that it took me to reach Maggie and Michael were like walking in no-man's-land. Counselling gave me personal power over my life. I was no longer a victim of my circumstances. I would take responsibility for whatever happened in my life from now onwards. But I still had a road to travel and decisions to make. My comfortable refuge in Chawton, that lovely village in Hampshire, would not solve my issues, and I was pulled out of there and reappointed to Clapham. I did not like that one little bit.

I could no longer take part in community life. I had no energy for it. I would do whatever I was asked to do, but it was hard going. I went out on some parish missions, preached as best I could and visited people, but there was little fire in me.

One of the first missions I went on at that time was to Leyton, in East London. I would go out in the evenings to visit people. One evening I came to a house and the man who answered the door to me seemed vaguely familiar.

'Have I met you before?' I asked him. A slow smile began to creep across his face.

'No,' he replied.

'Did I meet you outside church after Mass on Sunday?' I ventured, trying to work out exactly where I knew this face from.

'No,' he said. Then he added, 'You might have seen my face on television.' Then it began to dawn on me. I was face to face with Billy Power, one of the six men who had been wrongly convicted of the Birmingham bombings in 1974, and who had served 16 years in prison for something he had not done. As we sat and talked in his house I ventured to ask him, 'What was the overriding emotion that you felt when you were inside? Was it anger?'

'No,' Billy told me, 'it was frustration. When you are trying to tell somebody the truth and they are not listening to you – that is very frustrating, and that was the biggest thing when we were inside.'

One of the last missions I did was in Horley, near Gatwick Airport. It is memorable for a number of reasons. The parish priest was a lovely man called Michael Spelman. He was a County Mayo man, so that was a good start. I was losing the desire to keep going out knocking on the doors of strangers, and one day I asked Michael whether he minded if I stopped doing that. That was no problem to him. It was preaching and visiting the sick that he was concerned about. So that evening, on my final round of visiting, I found myself in the house of a couple from County Mayo, and after a pleasant meeting with them, I decided that this would be my last official house visit. It seemed appropriate to end with Mayo people.

In that parish there was a famous parishioner, the actor Michael Williams, husband of Judi Dench. Michael always left Mass just before the end so as not to get waylaid by anyone. He was a quiet, gentle person. As he emerged from Mass one Sunday morning, I happened to be strolling outside. I nodded to him, and he to me. Then, as he walked down the lane, I called to him. 'Michael!' He looked over to me. 'I liked *September Song*,' I called out. He smiled, waved and was gone. Michael and Russ Abbott had starred in that fine production.

I have another connection with Judi Dench. Her father was a doctor and, before Judi was born, he had a practice in Tyldesley, my native town. We all like to be connected to Judi!

One final story from that mission. Michael Spelman told me this: an elderly parish priest was being interviewed for a piece on Irish radio. The girl who came to interview him asked the old man to run through a typical day in his life. 'Well,' said the priest, 'I get up around eight o'clock and I go over and open the church. Then I come back and have a cup of tea. Later I go over for Mass at ten o'clock and talk to people. Then, when I come back here, Mary, the housekeeper, has the breakfast ready. Then I read the paper and open the mail.'

'What happens then?' asked the young reporter.

'Well, it is lunchtime then,' said the priest.

'And after that?'

'Well,' said the priest, 'after that, I shlacken off the resht of the day.' Wise man!

In 1996 I moved from Clapham to Sunderland to take over from the parish priest, John Brookes, who was dying of cancer. I was glad to move there, as it was a quiet place, and after the crowded atmosphere of Clapham, it would be a job I could do on my own. I realise now that I was mentally removing myself from religious life, even though I was not yet ready to physically do so.

This move to be a parish priest required me to obtain official status and approval from the bishop, a gentle Benedictine monk by the name of Ambrose Griffiths. He needed an assurance that my situation was not going to blow up before he appointed me, so Margaret was asked to sign a letter to that effect. She agreed to do so, because I asked her to, but she also made it clear to my superior that after this, she wished for us to be left alone to deal with our own issues, without any other interference! I remember my superior smiled when he read her letter, impressed by her power.

My time in Sunderland, in the parish of St Benet, Monkwearmouth, was a calm and pleasant time. The people there had a great sense of their own community and identity. I found them to be a warm and friendly people living on a cold shoulder of England! The parish was next door to Roker, where the old football stadium still stood when I arrived, and just a few minutes' walk from the bracing winds of the North Sea. The people there were very good to me, friendly and supportive. I even had a fan club of people who liked my sermons! They called themselves 'Father Fahy's Fulwell Fan Club'.

Looking back now at those final three years of my priesthood, I am very grateful that I ended my days there in Sunderland among those people. Although I carried a secret stress inside me, my days there were made easy and gentle by the human kindness that I found among those people. If they read these words of mine now, may they know that I remember them fondly and am eternally grateful for the days I spent among them.

I arrived in St Benet's as a fill-in for the parish priest, and I took over after he died. I was able to do all the things that needed to be done – Mass and visiting the sick being the important duties. But I had no drive, no ambition to launch out into any great service of the parish. I kept it ticking over.

When the day came for me to say goodbye to the people – I could not explain the details to them, obviously

– I gave an address at Mass in which I told them, 'There are two things that I am proud of in my time here. I have always done my best to preach well on every occasion, and I have always given my best attention to receive and to listen and talk with everyone who came to see me.'

These two issues are, in fact, the meat and drink of life every day for each person on earth. The first is the ability to speak openly and honestly, to speak for truth and for justice. We can all do that. The second is to be compassionate with every person we meet. We can all do that, too. These things constitute the two great commandments of life, the two great 'words' that really are our life.

I remember my father saying these things to me as we sat over a pint of beer at home in Lancashire. We were discussing how people can often be very troublesome, and my father took a sip of his ale and said in eloquent understatement, 'Ah, Brian, we all have our troubles, but no one has the right to be uncivil.' I think that is pure gold.

I was parish priest in Sunderland for three years before the day of freedom dawned for me. Margaret was patient with me all that time, more than I had any right to expect. In the end she sat down and wrote a letter to me to say that if I could not leave, then we had to let each other go. As Margaret was writing that letter, I was being formally asked by my superiors to make a decision about what I wanted my future to be.

I felt that this was the first time anyone had ever asked me properly what I wanted to do with my own life. It may sound strange, but that was truly how it felt. I heard the question clearly for the first time in my life. It had been put to me up front and openly. 'No one is stopping you, Brian. At this moment in your life, what do you want to do?' I could no longer avoid answering the question!

Up to this point no one had really put me on the spot with that question, and I had avoided asking myself in any way that would make me move! Now, John Trenchard, my superior, had put the question straight into my face. I am eternally grateful to John for this. When I told him later of his role in my leaving, he was bemused. He did not realise that he had done anything special. But he had. John has always been a very direct kind of guy, and it was the pure and simple honesty of his question that drew me out of the shadows of my life. That is how I read it today.

I went away to Ireland for nine days. This was a trip that I had already scheduled to visit my ageing mother, but now it became a personal retreat to try and answer the question John had put to me. How fitting that I should go back to Mayo, the land of my inner happiness, to bring my final battle with unhappiness to a close.

I told my mother that a new move was on the way, and I was being asked to consider what it might be. But I feel sure that she, like any good woman, sensed that the issue was much deeper than that. But this unhappiness of mine was not a subject that she and I could wander about in. We keep people well away from our unhappy hearts. So Mum, like the good mum she was, suffered for her son in silence and at a distance. After all, we cannot live our children's lives for them.

After a few words about crossroads and new directions, all conversations on the subject ceased. There was no more to be said, to anyone. I went on a trip to visit local chapels that were dotted around the Westport area. I have always liked visiting churches, but once inside those places I had nothing to say to the good Lord. Not a word. Later I remembered the story of Zechariah, the father of John the Baptist, and of how he was struck dumb for not believing the angel's message about the child about to be born (Luke 1:5-23). I was struck dumb in the face of the new life that was about to be born in me.

I came back to Sunderland and went for a pint with my friend Ed. Someone will say that it was Guinness that solved my problem, but even that dark and handsome brew is not that powerful. But I came home to the monastery after three pints 'and the ligament of his tongue was loosened and he spoke clearly' (Mark 7:35)! Suddenly, as if from nowhere, I began to say things.

The way was clear. The road was straight ahead. There was nothing to hold me back. I was going to go to Maggie and Michael. That was my next move. That was my new direction. Those nine days of brooding silence in Mayo had not been for nothing. They served as preparation for the new life about to be born.

EIGHT

Vows

Very soon after settling into my new life and home with Maggie and Michael, I applied formally for dispensation from the vows that I had taken in the Church: vows that I had taken as an 18-year-old to live my life in the religious order, and vows that I had made before the bishop on the day I was ordained a priest, at the grand old age of 23. Once you make these vows, you commit yourself for the rest of your life.

Such was our way of talking about these things, you would think that you were walking into a death sentence. But the vows were proposed to us as such serious and ultimate realities, it would be regarded as a sin to leave after taking them. And yet the Church encouraged young people to walk into them so easily. Then, once they were inside, it made it a virtual impossibility to escape from them!

When I first fell in love, in my early years of priesthood, and thought of leaving, or least of having some time out to think things through, I went home to see my parents. 'After all', I said to myself, 'if I am going to do this, to walk away from vows, I need to be able to look my own mother and father in the eye'.

My mother was beside herself with torment and could not believe that I would do such a thing. My father was gentler with me, but after a week of anguish, even he was near breaking point, wringing his wet handkerchief and saying through his tears, and in a voice that was all pleading and all compassion, 'But your vows, Brian, your vows.'

Yes, my vows! The man who had taken vows in religious life was no more than a child, a young boy of 18. The young man who had knelt before the bishop to make priestly vows was still only a boy. When I finally left, I wanted that truth to be admitted by the Church. I wanted that fact acknowledged. I wanted it to be made absolutely clear that if there was fault here, it lay with the institution that encouraged a child into this life, and not with me, for I had tried my level best, all my life, to follow the light. In leaving now to join my life to Maggie and Michael, I wanted a public avowal by the Church that it was a good and an honourable thing that I did.

The process of applying for dispensation required me to fill in a form outlining the story of my life, my curriculum vitae, and also my reasons for asking for dispensation. Testimonies from two witnesses were also submitted. I have one of those testimonies on my desk today. It was submitted by Edward Hone who at various times in my life has been a student, a fellow priest and a dear friend. Ed is the kind of friend who tells you straight! I know this from experience. I am a Lancashire man and Ed is a Yorkshire man. There is a difference . . .

Ed Hone's testimony reads as follows:

Introduction

I first met Brian Fahy in 1982 when he was giving a parish Mission near my home town of Bradford. I then knew Brian when I was a Redemptorist student and he was appointed rector of the house of formation in Canterbury. I have subsequently worked with Brian and have lived in community with him for a total of six years. Brian and I are friends, and I feel I know him well.

Life at a distance

When Brian was my superior in Canterbury, he lived life as though from a distance. He engaged with life only when it was demanded of him; for the rest of the time he appeared to suffer from a low-level depression. Little interested him or animated him. Whilst he was always friendly, generous and kind, he was essentially detached from the community life and academic environment in which he had found himself.

Brian's formation

Brian would often talk about his own Redemptorist formation, about how he went to the juvenate at the age of 11, how it was presumed that he would progress to the novitiate, which he duly did; and how he took vows and was subsequently ordained. He spoke about these stages of his life as things that happened to him, rather than as things he chose. It became clearer to me that he resented his lack of freedom of choice with regard to his life. His resentment was suppressed, and in my opinion, this led to his depression.

Why did Brian stay a Redemptorist?

From time to time when Brian was lamenting his lot in life, I would challenge him and suggest he leave the Congregation and/or the priesthood. Brian could not conceive of this as a possibility. He felt helpless; he said he had been institutionalised since the age of 11 and doubted very much if he would be able to negotiate life as a layman. He was fearful of leaving and unhappy in staying.

Brian was not meant to be a priest

Brian was always a good priest, in his dealings with people, in his interpretation of their lives, and in his preaching of the Gospel. He is kind, pastoral, thoughtful and articulate – but he was never meant to be a priest.

Brian's dilemma

Brian's dilemma was heightened when he met Margaret. Discovering subsequently that she was expecting a baby tore him apart emotionally. He was not under any direct pressure to leave the Redemptorists to be with Margaret and their soon-to-be-born child, and yet he longed to be with them. But he did not feel he had the personal authority over his own life to make the decision to leave his Religious life.

Impossible to leave the Redemptorists?

It was even more frustrating living with Brian from that time onwards. He was not engaged in community or apostolic life in any real sense – his heart was elsewhere. But he was not living with those he loved as he could not imagine leaving the priesthood.

The last three years

Brian's final three years of Redemptorist life were spent in Sunderland where he was superior of the community and parish priest. The style of community life was much less institutional, and much more domestic than he had been living previously. I think Brian felt less and less the demands of the institution of Religious Life; and consequently the call of a real life beyond it beckoned more powerfully.

Knowing he had a child whom he loved, and the mother of the child whom he also loved, eventually tipped the balance. Brian became what he should have been all along – a good husband (in all but name) and a good father.

Brian's vocation

Anyone who has known Brian associates with him the sadness he has lived with since the age of 11, when he began the unfree, inexorable path to Religious life and Priesthood. Without repudiating his ministry, indeed with a strong desire to continue it through the Redemptorist Publications apostolate, Brian, for the first time, has truly chosen his vocation in life.

I have kept in close contact with Brian, Margaret and Michael in the five months since Brian left the Redemptorists. He is happier than I have ever known him. Margaret, whom I have known for seven years, seems equally happy, as does Michael. The ease with which Brian has made a transition that at one time he could not even imagine, confirms for me that his choice has been the right one. His decision, made with Margaret at every stage, seems a mature one. He seems to be finding a fulfilment in life now that he has never found before.

Ed Hone CSsR

In the springtime of 2001 I received a document from the Vatican in Rome that gave me the dispensation that I sought. Whatever the reasoning of the judges in giving me this dispensation, my reasoning was clear. I had not exercised mature freedom in the commitment that I made when I was taking vows. If I were to put it more bluntly, I would say that the Church in its institutions, junior and senior seminary, deprived me of the normal upbringing that I was entitled to, in the bosom of my own family, friends and locality. They took me away from that family environment, and they considered what they were doing to be perfectly fine. And it wasn't! I was obedient, and I paid a price.

So when it came time to take vows again – this time the vows of marriage – I took my time about it. My childhood friend, David, once he had met Maggie, encouraged me to get married, but I needed some space, some psychological space first of all. I had spent a lifetime in vows. I needed just to be me, and to get the feel of what it was like to be me, before giving a commitment again. I did not doubt that I would. But that space was very important to me.

I was with Maggie and Michael for five years before I put the proposal to Maggie. I needed that time, that gap, in order to come to vows again in a mature and completely free manner. I proposed to Maggie in July and suggested to her that we get married in October! She had three months to get things ready, and she did. I picked the month of October because I saw that the sixteenth fell on a Saturday – a good day for a wedding – and 16 October was the exact date on which I had first taken religious vows. There was a message there that I wanted to give!

We had a lovely wedding day. Ed Hone came to officiate and did us proud. My brother Michael was my best man. Young Michael, our son, now 12 years of age, led his Mum up the aisle, wearing a splendid tartan kilt. My brother and I were equally kilted out. 'I never thought I'd see the day,' my brother said in his speech. 'Two bald-headed Lancastrians in kilts!'

There were 40 guests for the wedding breakfast and a gathering of 100 or so in the evening, when we all danced to the Ceilidh band, Clamjamfry, of my friend John Kelleher. I spoke in my speech about the day the train had pulled into Stirling railway station, about that little cosy kiosk, and about how Stirling had now become my happy home. 'I give you Maggie, Stirling and home!' was my toast.

Maggie and I went to Rome, courtesy of my childhood friend and travel agent entrepreneur, David, and spent a memorable honeymoon in the Eternal City. I really was letting them know!

My Mammy was too old to travel to the wedding, but she sent representatives. She asked me to make sure that my senior cousins in Manchester, the eldest children of her three sisters from the Manchester clan, should be invited and be there to ensure that the family was present at my belated wedding. That wish I was only too happy to fulfil, and so my cousins Raymond, Marion and Pauline all travelled from Manchester to witness and to take part in my wedding day.

On my computer screen as I write there is a photograph of my Mammy, looking out at me with her gentle smile, and holding our wedding album in her hands. The photograph was taken by Maggie, and there is in the corner of my mother's eyes a little moisture, the trace of tears: tears of joy for the happiness of her eldest boy, tears of sadness for the lost years, and a smile that seems to say to me, 'It's all right now.' Or, as her little boy would ask of her, 'Mammy, doadly shing?' Yes, Brian, that was a lovely song.

My life has become a lovely song, not a mournful melody. Even though I have lost my Maggie to sudden death, my life is a completed life, a fulfilled life, a life without complaint. What more on earth could I ever wish for? I was loved so much, as a child by my mother and my father, and by my two sisters and my brother, and by our collie dog. I was loved by my friends at home in Tyldesley, by my relations in Ireland and by friends in the Church along the way, despite the unseen issues. Most of all, I have been loved by Maggie, and by my own dear son. What on earth have I to complain about?!

People have written to me since my Maggie died, and they have said to me how blessed, how fortunate I am to have known love. For, they say, many people go through life and never know love. If this be so, then I pray God help them. For we cannot live if we are not loved. And we cannot be happy if we do not find someone ourselves to love.

A vow is a solemn promise, or maybe we should say it is a simple promise to love someone. It is a gift of oneself to another person. In this sense, it is a beautiful thing to do. But in order to do it, we need to know who we are. We also need the strength and the support that comes from the life we live with other people. That is why childhood is so important. In childhood we start to learn who we are.

I knew from the very first moment of my existence that I was loved. My father held me in his arms, sat me on his knee and sang to me. My mother embraced me and kissed me and hugged me, and she fed me and warmed me and cuddled me and told me how she would love me forever. Never in my life, for one minute, did I ever feel anything from my mother but the most absolute love and devotion. Isn't it time to say that?! To look back at the story and at the journey of my life and to say my mother was absolutely wonderful to me.

The vows that my mother took, standing before the altar at Saint Cuthbert's church in Didsbury, Manchester, on 15 April 1944, vows spoken to one Michael Fahy, included not only a promise of love for life but also the implicit promise of mothering the children that might be born to them in the course of their life together. That vow and that promise she kept to the utmost of her ability every day of her long life – a life that lasted for 94 years.

My father, I know, never said anything during the years of my religious training. He left that department to my mother. He felt that mothers knew best where children are concerned. That was part of the generation he grew up in.

I remember the day of the junior school sports, when I had won everything in sight – races, long jump, high jump and relay – and my father had come out early from the pit to watch me. As we came away from the sports field and I was carrying my medals and cups, my father walked quietly beside me. I remember wanting him to put his hand on my shoulder, but he did not do so. Years afterwards I told this story to my mother.

'That was the way he was brought up,' Mammy explained to me. 'They weren't very good at showing their feelings in those days. Life was hard and they just got on with it. But don't worry, Brian, your father was very proud of you.'

I know from his silences and from conversations in later life, again from the things that he did not say, that my father kept his own counsel where the Church was concerned, just as in the army he kept his own counsel where senior ranks where concerned. He gave due respect to his superiors in religion and in the army, and kept his own views to himself.

If pushed to give a view, I am sure he would have wanted me to stay at home. But then, I think my mother would have wanted that too. But Mum, good Irish Catholic girl that she was, was prepared to follow the Church's bidding and to make the sacrifice, and Dad was prepared to leave the upbringing of the children to Mum. If I had been allowed to stay at home and grow up there, it would have been the better way of it. I missed my mum and my dad. I missed all my family in those growing-up years, and as the years went by, I thought I had missed out on life. But in the end I didn't. And I have Maggie to thank for that.

NINE

Visiting Mammy

In 1994 my Mammy returned to Ireland to live in a granny flat beside my sister Tricia, near the lovely town of Westport in County Mayo. She was 78 years old, and she would live another 16 years there in the West of Ireland. I visited her every year, as I had done all through my life, and when I left the priesthood and joined my life to Maggie's, those visits continued, but now I came as a family man, and not on my own.

I had been visiting my Mammy all my life. The little boy started coming home from the age of 11, and that pattern continued until the day she died. There is, naturally, a special kind of relationship between a priest and his mother, quite simply owing to the fact that a priest does not marry, and does not have another woman in his life. He has not left his father and mother and joined himself to his wife, and so that bond of mother and son can remain very strong. That is the way it was with us. And given the fact that I went away so young, and into the religious life before my own adult development had happened, the mother–son ties were very strong indeed.

But they were not unhealthy. My own personal development certainly needed attention, and any unhealthiness, I submit, lay in that area, and perhaps made me more connected to my mother than I otherwise would have been. And when I met Maggie and made my life with her, the balance of my relationship with my mother was settled very clearly on an even keel.

My mother, too, was very aware of the closeness we shared, and she would often make a joke of it by referring to one of Alan Bennett's *Talking Heads,* where a mother and son have a very strong connection. In 'A Chip in the Sugar', the mother and son often go out visiting ancient monuments on their days out, as I did with my mum. Quoting the final lines of the monologue, where the main character, Graham, and his mum are about to set off for Ripon cathedral, my mum would say, 'We like old buildings, don't we, you and I?' She was all there, my mother.

In her young married days, Mum had made the trip to Ireland almost every year with her young, growing family to visit her own beloved mother who was herself a very strong woman. Separated by the necessity of emigration, my mother crossed the sea every year to embrace her mother.

One time, as a young woman, after her second visit home, Mammy wondered if her mother would accompany her to Ballina Railway Station to see her off once more to Manchester and to domestic service, as she had done previously. 'No,' said her mother, with tears in her eyes. 'I don't want to see that big black monster taking you away from me.' Now, in her old age, Mum was settled back on the west coast of Ireland, and it was my turn to make those journeys, to see her and spend time with her.

With Maggie and Michael, I took Mum out again to visit the places that we had toured during the early years of my priestly life. Mayo is dotted with old ruined abbeys, as well as fierce coastal cliffs in the north and peaceful sandy beaches in the west. We revisited them all.

Not far from her Westport home is the restored and beautiful abbey of Ballintubber, a particular favourite of my mother's. Ballintubber is a wonderful place, where Mass has been celebrated uninterrupted for a thousand years. The roofless church was restored and, in the early days of my priestly life, Mum and I met Father Egan, the great administrator of that renovation. He now lies buried in the shadow of that ancient church, and Mum and I paid our respects on our visits there. There is a modern-day pilgrimage that starts from Ballintubber and, using an ancient pathway, leads all the way to the conical mass of Croagh Patrick, Ireland's holy mountain, whose distinctive shape can be seen from the abbey, standing proudly on the horizon.

One Sunday afternoon during our summer holiday visit, we took Mum out for dinner to a hotel in the town. As the meal was ending, and as I thought to take her home again to her little house, I asked her if there was anything she would like to do. 'I'd love to go to Ballintubber,' she said. I was not expecting this, as it would mean two trips in that direction, one for the visit, and one to reach the little cottage where we were staying for the duration. Maggie laughed at my surprise, but it was a fine sunny day, so what was the problem?!

Mum loved that visit, and as she stood in the grounds of the abbey, I could see in her eyes the multitude of memories flooding back to her of earlier visits to this tranquil spot. It was her last visit, and I think she knew it. Maggie took a photo to record the occasion.

But of all the fine places we ever visited, most of all Mum loved to go back to Erris, to that wild western corner of the county where life had begun for her, and to visit the area 'inside Belmullet', the peninsula down as far as Blacksod and Faulmore. This is a very special place; it is like being at the edge of the world. The sea creeps in all around you. To the south stands the imposing bulk of Slievemore, the mountain on Achill Island. Out in front is a scattering of islands – Duvillaun and Inishkea – where people lived until the 1930s. Ten fishermen were drowned in a boating tragedy in 1927, and a mass grave lies behind in the ancient cemetery site of Saint Dervla's Well at Faulmore. Up the coast can be seen the low-lying island of Inishglora, a site of sixth-century Christianity that contains monastic cells and ancient crosses.

Mary Robinson, the former president of Ireland, herself a native of Mayo, tells a story of being on the islands of Inishkea on 11 September 2001. As planes were targeting the Twin Towers of New York, causing death and destruction and pouring sulphuric gloom over our sorry world, Mary was in the stillness, the quiet peacefulness of an Irish morning on those sainted islands. What a contrast of life. The world as it so sadly is, and the world as we would love it to be.

One evening in September 2008 Mum was talking on the phone to my sister Sheila, who lives in a picture-postcard cottage by the sea outside Westport. Mum got up to turn off the radio, so as to talk more peacefully, and promptly fell over. She broke her hip. This marked the beginning of the end for her. She went through an operation to have a hip replacement. Then she went through another operation for a cataract on her eye, but very soon she found herself needing full-time care, and so she was admitted to the Sacred Heart Hospital in Castlebar. She lived there, a gentle and patient resident, for a year. The lady who had so patiently and so lovingly tended old people in Astley Hospital 40 years before, the lady who had charge of an old people's home 30 years before, now needed full-time care herself. She knew the score. She knew the drill. She knew the lie of the land. She was patience itself.

My son Michael and I came over to visit her in Castlebar. Maggie, by this time, could not come, as her own health issues were becoming somewhat serious. She had been diagnosed with a rare form of lung disease and had been told that her life expectancy was less than two years. She had signed up to the transplant list and was now at home with oxygen by her side. While Mum was in her hospital bed, Maggie went through her lung transplant operation – a miracle of medical treatment that would allow her to visit Ireland once more.

While Maggie was recuperating from her operation, Michael and I made our trip over to the west. During one of our visits to Castlebar hospital, the nurses needed some time to see to Mum, so I took Michael on a special journey, a half-hour scenic drive up the road via Pontoon where the two lakes of Lough Conn and Lough Cullen meet. We were going to a place called Barnfield, Knockmore, to see the old house where my Auntie Mary and cousin Mike Walsh used to live. I had spent many happy holidays in that house. Now the old ones were gone and the house, looking spick and span as a holiday home for the wider family, was closed up. We walked around the old place and looked in at the windows. And I remembered days gone by.

I remembered an evening with cousin Mike, a bachelor farmer some years older than me. We went down to the local pub, Brogan's in Knockmore, and enjoyed a few jars. Sitting at the end of the bar on a high stool, I had a perfect view of the pints of Guinness being poured and allowed to settle on the inner shelf, before being topped. A black and white regiment. They weren't on parade for very long before being sent over the top!

As the night wore on, Mike asked me if I would mind giving a lift home to an elderly man at his side. 'No problem,' I said, and when it was time to go, the three of us left together. I drove slowly up the road in the dark of night, and turned right when instructed into a narrow boreen. As we approached the old man's cottage, I heard a dog bark – a bark of welcome for its owner. The old man, a widower, thanked us for the lift, got out of the car and went into his little house, set among quiet fields.

'Do you know what he'll do now?' Michael asked me. 'He'll make himself a bite to eat and sit before his turf fire for a while, himself and the dog. Then he'll go to bed and sleep till mid-morning. His land is leased to a neighbour, now that he is old. Tomorrow he will make his way back to the village where his daughter lives and he will have his dinner there, and tomorrow night he will call into Brogan's again.'

I thought of this gentle old man and this routine of his at the end of his days, here in the quiet Irish countryside. Then I thought of Mike, my cousin, sitting beside me as we motored home. Soon he will be an old man on his own, living in his own little place. And Mike, too, has a dog to bark a welcome.

After a year or so in Castlebar hospital, Mum got the move we wanted for her, back to Westport and into the care home there, the McBride Nursing Home. She arrived there on 20 August 2009, the day on which we had always celebrated her birthday. She was to live happily in that home for another year and two months.

Mum's energy was all gone now, and she needed help with everything, but her mind always remained clear, and her ability to recite the poems that had entertained me as a child was as strong as ever. Lying there in her bed, slightly propped up, she would launch into John Locke's poem, 'Dawn on the hills of Ireland'. I would stand at the end of the bed, looking down on my wonderful mother, as she quietly and assuredly recited the verses one by one:

> Now fuller and truer the shoreline shows.
> Was there ever a scene so splendid?
> I feel the breath of the Munster breeze.
> Thank God that my exile's ended!
> Old scenes, old songs, old friends again,
> the vale and cot I was born in
> O Ireland up from my heart of hearts,
> I bid you the top of the morning!

With the rising and the falling of her voice, I was transported once again to those holidays of childhood, to that boat out on the Irish Sea, and to those blissful times we spent in the fields of Erris.

In the summer of 2010 I visited Mum for the last time. I knew that I would not see her again in this world, but I did not make a drama out of it. I kissed her as she lay in her bed, and I spoke softly into her ear. 'Mammy,' I said. 'We are all in the hands of God.'

She looked at me gently and replied, 'Yes, Brian, we are all in the hands of God.' That was what my mother had told me all my life, and I accept it as the truth of life. I would not separate myself from her now by saying that she was going and I was staying in this world. We all have to make the journey through the gateway of death, passing through individually, but we do not need to feel alone, or be left alone. It will be the same for all of us, so it is something that we should assist each other to do.

I can see my mother's face now as I write this, looking back at me from her bed as I stand at the door of her room and look back at her lovely face. In leaving her, I knew that I was leaving her in the loving care of my sisters and nephews. They visited all the time. My nephew, Robert, would even bring Bruce, the big beast of a dog that he had, down to the home and tie him outside by the window so that even the dog could look in and visit my mum.

On the night she died, I was at home in Stirling. I put my mobile phone beside my bed, knowing that a call would likely come in the small hours. At 1.20am the phone rang. As I lifted it to my ear, I heard sobbing at the other end. It was my sister, Tricia. She was keeping vigil with Robert that night, after relieving Sheila earlier. From the midst of the sobbing I heard Tricia's voice. 'She's gone, Brian,' she sobbed. 'She's gone.'

Maggie had woken and I told her the news. I phoned my brother to tell him and then I went downstairs and made a cup of tea, and sat quietly in the kitchen for a short while. My mother's long life, her lovely life was over. I felt no anguish, only peace. And as I do in all situations, happy or sad, easy or stressful, I went back to bed, closed my eyes and sought my strength in sleep.

TEN

The Big Turn

The Stena ship sailed out from Stranraer Harbour and headed for Belfast Lough. It was a beautiful October day. Blue, blue sky and bright, bright sunshine, and not a cloud to be seen. Maggie, Michael and I were making our last visit to Mammy, for her funeral mass and burial. We drove down from Belfast as far as a place called Fivemiletown and stayed the night in the Valley Hotel in that spot in County Tyrone. I remember that the sun was shining directly into my eyes all the way from Belfast to our destination that evening, a bright yellow and orange sun. It was indeed the sunset on my mother's long life. Ninety-four years she had lived, a life full of health, vigour and love for all her children and grandchildren.

I thought my mother's death would cause me great upset and sorrow, given the closeness of the bonds of love between us, but that was not the case. As I stood on the ship sailing out of Stranraer, I felt a deep peace in my soul, a happiness even, that my mother's wonderful life had come to a gentle close. Mammy always said that each stage of life prepares you for the next one, and her long life and its gradual fading seem to have prepared her children, too, for the day of her leaving us.

And yet, an audible shock came from me when I walked into the room where my Mammy's body was laid out in her coffin. The sight momentarily unnerved me, but then I was OK. My son Michael cried to see me upset, as well as at seeing his beloved grandmother lying there.

Tricia had arranged my Mammy's house and room beautifully. There was a rocking chair in the corner, and her walking stick, which she used when going down the boreen for exercise. There were candles, photographs and flowers. It was like walking into a chapel.

Some cousins came to pay their respects the day before the funeral as they would not be able to be present for the Requiem Mass. We stood around beside my mother's coffin and spoke warmly to one another. We had not seen one another for a good few years and yet, because of all those childhood holidays, we felt like brothers and sisters. We recalled our grandparents, my mother's parents, and how they were greatly separated in age, grandfather being a good 20 years older than our grandmother. 'But that was the way of it in those days,' my cousin Tony said.

'Yes,' I agreed, thinking of the age difference between me and my own Maggie – a gap of 18 years. 'Yes, that was the way of it, and now I am reviving the tradition!'

On the morning of Mammy's funeral, the heavens opened and torrential rain poured from the skies all morning long. I have never seen the like of it. Umbrellas and long raincoats did the trick for us as we walked in procession behind the coffin down the street of the town and into St Mary's Church in Westport. My priest friend, Ed, presided at the Mass, and after his sermon I got up to say a few words by way of a eulogy.

When I left the priesthood, one of the things that Mammy said to me in the course of our rambling conversations was, 'I always thought you would do my funeral.'

Under the understandable stress of trying to explain things to Mum, I replied, 'Mum, I did not become a priest in order to do your funeral!' But I am happy to say that Mum got her wish. I may not have been the presiding priest at the Mass, but I did get up to the pulpit – a place that I always liked – and I spoke to the gathered congregation about our beloved Mammy.

I recalled her beloved Glen, and that journey we had made so often long ago as a family, coming home to visit our relations. And I remembered that day of leaving at the holiday's end, when the tears started and we all cried, and of sitting in the car as Daddy drove away, when we came to that spot in the road that we know as the 'Big Turn'. That is the point where the vision began and ended: seeing the homestead for the first time as we approached; losing sight of it once more as we headed away for another year.

Mammy has gone round the 'Big Turn' in the road, I told the congregation. Gone now beyond our sight. Gone to God in whom she believed so fervently and so lovingly. There will be great reunions there to rejoice in.

I ended my address by recalling the most wonderful thing our Mammy ever said to us children. It was like a mantra. She said it often and she lived up to its promise all her life. Wrapping us in her arms in warm towels after our Saturday night baths, Mammy would hold us and say to each one of us, 'I'll love you today, and I'll love you tomorrow, and I'll love you for all the years to come.' No towel, no fireside glow could be any warmer than the words that she uttered then.

We came out of church and we were greeted by more of our Carey cousins, and the pouring rain was still going strong. At Aughval cemetery, south west of Westport town, the rain stopped, and we lowered my Mammy's mortal remains into that gentle earth. I have been back there many a time since, always with Maggie, my beloved wife, and prayed at the grave, and enjoyed the beauty and the peace of the place. I have felt near to heaven in that quiet spot.

For the reception we all went back to the Clew Bay Hotel for hot and nourishing food, and the gentle day played itself out with a quiet pint as the night drew on. Four years earlier, in that same hotel, the family had gathered to celebrate Mammy's ninetieth birthday, and on that occasion she had looked very much the lady she always was. I had written one of my poems, recording her life story, and I read it out to her. It was based upon the rhythms of an old Irish song, 'Moonlight in Mayo'.

Maggie sat beside her that day, and the two of them went off to the ladies' room together like two old friends, which they now were. Both are now gone from me. My own Maggie has also gone round the 'Big Turn', out of sight, and I miss her very much.

Mammy was a great one for a good line of observation. On that day of her birthday celebration, she watched the smokers in the gathering go outside the dining room onto a balcony that overlooks the Carrowbeg River that flows through Westport town. As they gathered outside for a smoke, Mum turned to Maggie and said, 'Look at them now, just like cows in a field before bad weather!'

Across the river, across from that balcony, stands the McBride Nursing Home, and the window of the room in which my Mammy would breathe her last breath is clearly visible. But that was still four years away. We do not know what is ahead of us, and when you think about it, thank God that it is so! If we knew the future, we would never get out of bed in the mornings, for we would see all the problems and challenges that lie ahead, and we would feel ill equipped to face them; we would not want to know. But life comes at us piecemeal, in daily doses, and we are well able for that. Does not the good Lord tell us, 'Do not worry about tomorrow: tomorrow will take care of itself. Each day has enough trouble of its own' (Matthew 6:34).

I remember now the first time I was ever called out, as a young priest, to the bed of a dying man. It was 1971. Across the road from the monastery in Clapham and down a side lane, in an old property long since pulled down, an old Irishman lay dying. I had been called out by his neighbour, and at 2am in the morning I found myself in this little flat.

I began to stumble though some prayers in the book that I had with me, when suddenly the old man chirped up, 'Father, are you not going to hear my confession?' It was a request, a rebuke and a kind directive all in one. I shut my book and sat down beside him and let him pour out his love of God in his sorrow for his sins. I have never forgotten that old man. There was I at the beginning of a long road in priestly life, and there was he at the end of his long journey through this world. Our paths crossed in the middle of that night. He made his peace with God with the help of a stumbling young gossoon of a priest, and then was taken by ambulance out of his last home in this world. I never saw him again. Isn't it strange, the things you never forget?!

A few years later, still in Clapham, I was called out in the middle of the morning to a young couple who had found their little baby dead in the cot that morning.

I remember walking up Kings Avenue in Clapham looking for their address, and going in to a totally still and silent house.

The young father took me through to a room where a dead child lay in a cot. I took out my book and I prayed slowly over the child, and I touched the child on its forehead with oil. Back in the main room, the mother sat inconsolable in one chair. The father sat in another part of the room, also inconsolable, and I sat down in another chair in another part of the room. And I said nothing. I sat in stillness and silence with them for a long time. Then at some point I said to them that I would go and arrange things through the undertaker and would see them again.

I thank God that my instinct was good and guided me to behave and to do the right thing that day. Words would have been out of place. Silence and presence was all that was needed.

The death that made me cry was my father's. He died in hospital, five days after being admitted from home. We were all there during those days, Mum, myself, Tricia, Sheila and Michael Gerard. In many ways he was still young, at 71, but his lungs had taken a battering from coalmines, from pneumonia as a soldier, from warfare and rough conditions, from coalmines again and from a lifetime of smoking.

He died in my mother's arms, being lifted by a nurse in order to take a sip of water. It was too much for him; he had no breath left, and he died. I had left my mother at the hospital to go and phone the rest of the family, and when I returned and was told my father had died, I just burst into a flood of tears. My mother passed me a tissue and, misunderstanding her kindness, I told her to let me be and to let me cry. I did not know I had so many tears.

I think it was the suddenness of his passing that took us all unaware, despite our familiarity with his chronic condition. And, of course, it was my first experience of the loss of somebody close to me. I still remember looking out of a huge plate-glass window in the office of the undertaker later that day and seeing a panorama of my home town, and even the street where my father had been born 71 years earlier. The world is exactly the same place I always knew, I said to myself, but now it is also totally different. Now I have to live in this world without the kind and gentle presence of my father. There was a real sense of having to be more responsible, a sense that the mantle had been passed on and laid across my shoulder.

ELEVEN

The line of your life

My mother would spend 22 years of her life as a widow, living in her own house by herself for nearly all of that time. Her own mother, my grandmother, Bridget Carey, was a widow for 42 years, from 1920 when her husband Anthony died, until the May of 1962. What a change came over the world during the course of those years, from the shock and the devastation that followed World War I, through years of the Depression, through World War II, and through the quiet fifties. Nan saw her children grow up and leave her and go off to another country, to that land across the sea where the terrible war was going on.

Four of her girls went over to Manchester to find work and eventually to find husbands. Two of her daughters stayed in Ireland. One of them – Sarah – stayed in the Glen, maybe a mile away. One son, Hugh, stayed on the land and reared his own family there. He was only 11 when his father died, and he had to play the man. The other son, John, was something of a poet and a maker of verses. He went to England and married a Protestant lady by the name of Nancy Lee, a thing which, I feel, must have caused a problem in the Catholic Ireland of those days, and which became something of an unspoken story in the family.

Settling down in the Bishop's Stortford area, John reared a family of five fine boys, but he lost contact with his siblings over the years, and never saw his mother again. When the telegram came to say that his dear mother was dying, John took it and sat in a corner of his house by himself and quietly mourned the mother that he had loved so much.

As a child, I remember seeing at home a simple photograph of five boys, standing all in a line, and asking my mother about them. 'They are your cousins, the children of your Uncle John, and they live a long way away,' Mammy told me. I found this information very strange to accept. I knew all my cousins – those in Manchester, and those in Ireland – and they lived a long way away. How come I do not get to see these five boys?

I grew up not knowing this branch of my family, although in conversation with my mum it was very clear how much she loved and missed her brother John.

In the summer of 1980, I happened to be in Bishop's Stortford, attending an ordination, so I took the opportunity to visit the hamlet of Great Hallingbury, where Uncle John and Aunt Nancy lived. I met a gentle and a quiet man that day, but I have no recollection of our conversation, only that I was welcomed and warmly received.

One cold and snowy winter, 18 months later, Uncle John died, days after losing his beloved Nancy. Mammy and her sister Bea attended Nancy's funeral, and they must have had a powerful reunion with their brother in that moment. It was only matter of a few days before John, too, followed his Nancy. My Mammy said to me that he died of a broken heart, not wanting to live when Nancy died. Still a priest in those days, I went to the village church, and the local vicar gave me great welcome, and we conducted my Uncle John's funeral together.

It was religion that caused the trouble for my uncle John and his Nancy, and caused a distance to develop between John and his siblings. John never saw his own dear mother again, and they loved each other dearly. Twenty years went by until the day that telegram arrived for John, saying, 'Come home. Mother dying.'

It would be a few more years before John did, in fact, go home. He visited the Glen and met with his brother, Hugh, and his sisters, Mary and Sarah. My own visit to John, when I was still a priest and dressed in black, seems to me now to be some kind of apology to my beloved uncle on behalf of the Church, whose strict and rigid rules about marriage had caused such family problems, and which caused estrangement to happen between people who loved each other so tenderly. I am so glad, looking back now, that I was able to be present for my Uncle John's funeral, and to pray his soul to God.

It is two years and more now since my mother died, and I find myself now thinking about the line of her life. She started out in life as a wee girl. 'Baby Ellen' she was called. Then she was a schoolgirl. Then she became a young woman, then an emigrant and a worker for wages, then a young wife who could so easily have become a widow in those war-torn years, if my father's fate had not been kind. Then she became a young mother, then a working nurse, then a matron of a care home for the elderly in Wigan, and for three brief years a lady in retirement with Dad. Then she became a widow for 22 years, and a wonderful granny and always a wise lady. Most of all she was a mother, and that vocation never ended until she finally closed her eyes. This is the lifeline of my mother, briefly told.

This is a great lesson to us. In the course of our life we are many things, and we figure in many relationships.

Our influence in the lives of others is far more powerful than we often realise. The line of my own life has taken on many characteristics since the little boy who went away to boarding school. I became a student, a baby-priest, a preacher, a teacher, a listener, a lost soul. Then after meeting Maggie I became a father, a husband, a mediator, a writer and now, as I write this, I am learning what it is to be a widower. Some of these roles are temporary experiences, some very long-lasting indeed. But once a parent, always a parent. That relationship is a lifetime connection and commitment. And for those who lose contact with children, it is a lifetime of pain and sorrow.

The love I have received in my lifetime will last me forever. Where I am now, the balance can be shifted from needing love to giving love more. Surrounded by a mother's love, and a father's love, and that of siblings, family and friends, I am rich indeed. And the day I met my Maggie and fell in love with her just lifted my whole life into orbit. So I have every reason now to give to others what has been so abundantly given to me.

My experiences in my work in family mediation bring me into face-to-face contact with parents who are now separated. Some of them manage things tolerably, but for all of them it is a painful and a stressful world that they live in. What greater pain is there than to be separated from your children, even for a few nights, even when they are being cared for by the other parent? The break-up of family life and its many consequences is the dominant heartbreaking narrative of our world.

By contrast, the story of my clan, of the people I come from, is a story of human togetherness. That is not to say that we have been spared the fractures and the follies that beset us all in this world. It is simply to relate how blessed I feel in the background and the people that I come from. This togetherness was most powerfully celebrated in the summer of 2012 when my mother's clan, the Careys of Glencullen, organised and celebrated a cousins' reunion over the August bank holiday weekend – 3, 4 and 5 August.

It began with a casual conversation that I had with my cousin, Kathleen Carey, now a retired teacher. Kathleen came to visit us the day before my Mammy's funeral. As she was leaving that afternoon, she made the comment about how we only meet at funerals these days, and wouldn't it be good if we were to organise a get-together on some occasion apart from that. 'Yes, it would, Kathleen,' I said to her. 'But it needs a driver, and you seem to me to be the kind of person who could organise it.' She did!

On the weekend of the August bank holiday, 50 of us descended on the townland of Glencullen Lower, Bangor Erris, Ballina, County Mayo, Ireland – children from the eight families, the Mayo and Manchester Mafia.

The occasion was well planned. It began on the Friday evening with an assembly in Bangor, where people mingled and shared photographs, and one spokesperson from each family gave an introduction to their particular branch. This was done especially for the benefit of Uncle John's children, three of whom were present with their wives. Uncle John's children were the 'lost tribe of Israel' in our story. They had had no trips to Ireland, no contact with the rest of us until our adult years. Now we were going to put that right.

On the Saturday lunchtime, we all gathered in the Glen and were shown the lie of the old house. We told stories of the old people, of our childhood visits and of our childhood memories. Then we put our boots on and took a walk down as far as the Lake and back again, mixing with one another and sharing stories again. At six o'clock we reassembled in the house of our childhood summers and shared a most wonderful meal, prepared for us by the resident Careys, all the while keeping a watchful eye, through the television, on the Mayo footballers, who were hunting for glory again. As the evening closed in, Maggie and I, my two sisters and my brother and their spouses made our way back into Bangor and sat down in the Kiltane Tavern for a welcome pint of the black stuff. Bangor is a quiet enough spot but, my word, it was lively enough! People must come back to it from all over the world!

Next morning, after a leisurely breakfast, my brother Michael, his wife Allison, Maggie and I went for a drive around by Broadhaven Bay and looked over to the coastline of Carrowteigue, where the sea sweeps gently into the land. On our way, we passed the old school house and I saw an old gentleman getting out of a car there. This was the famous Kenneth Whitaker, of Irish Economy fame, the owner and resident of the old school house, now a sprightly 92. I said hello to him and told him my business. I had met him years before with my mother and my aunt, Sarah, and he had graciously given us a conducted tour of his house at that time.

'I am here for a weekend reunion of the Careys of Glencullen,' I told the old man.

'And you're looking well on it!' was his reply.

That afternoon, the clan reassembled in Kiltane Graveyard where our grandfather had been buried in 1920. The ruin of a twelfth-century church stands there, among the heaped-up graves, and it seemed to welcome us into its embrace that day. As we began our reflections, readings and prayers, a light swish of rain swept across the roofless church, moistening our shoulders – heaven's gentle tears for the departed.

My cousin John, the eldest son of Uncle John, a quiet and gentle man of 69 years, opened his King James Bible and read in his quiet and attentive voice, 'To every thing there is a season, and a time to every purpose under the heaven' (Ecclesiastes 3:1). Other contributions were made, readings and poems. I had prepared a piece which I had written the week before, a letter to my grandfather. This is what I said.

Anthony Carey

You caught a chill, they tell me. Out saving hay.
A few months only and you died, 67 years of age.
My mammy never knew you, since she was only three.
Mary would have known you, but I never thought
to ask,
and John was 15 when you died, and I only saw
him once.

Katie, too, and Uncle Hugh, 13 and 11,
I never asked them about you, maybe their
children know.
But this I know quite simply:
you married Biddy Carey and were father of
eight children.

You lived at the time of the Land League, of Davitt
and Parnell.
You were a young man in your twenties at the time of
the Phoenix Park murders.
The Congested Districts Board was set up to parcel out
the land,
Sinn Fein and Home Rule was now the go,
and as the century turned you got married and had
your own home rule,
or did you?

From '03 to '18 a family grew on the land,
and just when you were needed most, you died.
From that day you became a memory,
buried out in Kiltane.
But you are more than that.

You are my grandfather.
Something of you is in me,
and I believe the promise that one day we shall meet.

You never had the joy of holding your grandchildren
in your arms.
But here today those same children gather to
embrace you.
I hope you are proud of us,
Anthony Carey.

I signed it 'Brian Fahy, 31 July 2012'.

When the readings were done, we climbed through an ancient narrow doorway to see a carved-out stone, a holy water stoop. We came away together, all of us feeling the power of having attended the funeral service of our grandfather, buried in that holy spot 92 years before.

Our next port of call was the modern graveyard outside Bangor where our grandmother, Bridget Carey, lies buried. Two of her children now lie buried nearby – Hugh and Sarah. Again, a member from each family came forward to tell a story, and it was there that we learned about the day our Uncle John received the telegram informing him of his mother's death. How quietly his son told us the story! How powerfully we heard it told!

The weekend was like an open canvas onto which each person laid a brushwork of paint, story on story, some solemn, some hilarious, some just quiet and simple memories. Like my brother Michael who told of sitting outside the gable end of the house as a small child, on a little ledge that jutted out from the wall, Nan sitting beside him, running her fingers through his blond hair and murmuring, 'Just like Tony.' Tony, our elder cousin, was the eldest grandson in Nan's house and a favourite of hers.

Over the weekend we, cousins together, blended all these stories into a rich tapestry, bringing our own understanding of our common story into much sharper relief and vivid colour. As the weekend drew to a close, the finale was a meal together in a fine restaurant near the town of Belmullet, just ten miles away. Moving pictures on the wall showed us familiar faces and happy times, and at each round table, each one of the eight families assembled and rejoiced in the scene.

Again, as the meal ended, a spokesperson got up to tell a story, this time of our own parents, and we all enjoyed the listening. A little boy sang for us. And then came Sophie.

Sophie was 5. She was the great-granddaughter of Sarah, the youngest of the Carey clan that we had just celebrated. Sophie lived in London and she had battled cancer for most of her life. As we were gathering for that final meal, our weekend of celebrations now completed, young Sophie died. They kept the news from us until the meal was over, so as not to halt proceedings, but then we were told, and a sorrowful silence descended upon us.

My cousin, Kathleen, asked me to speak after this news. I reflected on what we had done that weekend and about all the people who had gone before us, and whose memory we had celebrated. To that list of fine people, our forebears, we now added young Sophie. She was one of us. We belong to one another.

I expressed my simple and utter belief in the resurrection of the dead and the life of the world to come, the faith I first received at my mother's knee, and I professed my fervent belief in Jesus Christ. And we prayed the 'Our Father' and the 'Hail Mary' and prayed for eternal rest and for everlasting light to shine on Sophie now.

We began the weekend thinking especially of our grandmother, the old lady that we all knew as 'Nan', and whose days in this world were many. We ended it thinking about a smiling little girl whose days in this world were few. Bridget and Sophie.

TWELVE

Guiding spirits

When I was a student at senior seminary, aged 21, I came across a book of poems by Robert Burns, the Scottish bard. I liked what I read, and over the years Burns has never failed to attract and inspire me. The parallels and the differences between us I find amusing now. I was a dark-haired and good-looking man in my youth, as was Burns. Religion was a huge part of my life, as it was in the life and society of Burns. But Burns had access to the lassies, and I did not, and therein lay the big difference!

Everyone who reads Burns can readily agree with him when he takes a pop at religion, for the particular brand of Christianity that was inflicted upon him was a dour, severe and life-restricting Presbyterianism. The teaching that the Kirk put abroad was very negative about the human condition, and Burns would not tolerate it. He had a fire for life, and in a letter that he wrote to a friend, Burns speaks of his belief in human goodness and of his compassion for human beings in their weakness:

> God knows I am no saint: I have a whole host of follies and sins to answer for; but if I could, and I believe I do it as far as I can, I would wipe away all tears from all eyes.[7]

Burns puts human goodness first and human weakness and human sinfulness second, and he is right so to do. That is the gospel of Jesus Christ. But it is a balance that is

---

7. Letter to Mr Hill, *Bookseller*, 1790.

often hard to maintain, and it reminds me of my own religious upbringing and of the Catholic culture of my childhood days. We were often reminded of our sinfulness, and going to confession was a regular practice, reinforcing by 'doing' what the teaching was putting into our minds. It could cause some people to become somewhat repressed in their nature and somewhat uncertain about having a good time.

Of course, our Catholic ethos was also filled with warm and even romantic feelings about God, and the hymns we sang were often lovely melodies. I can hear those voices in Hindsford church to this day. The church was always filled with colour, flowers, candles and incense, all of which enticed the senses and spoke of a loving, warm-hearted God. Every morning when, as an altar boy, I led the priest on to the sanctuary for Holy Mass, we passed by the statue of the Sacred Heart of Jesus, and you could not get any warmer than that in your understanding of the love of God. So God's great love for us, and the hammered-home truth that we were sinful people, fought a never-ending duel for supremacy in the soul.

In my own personal Catholic consciousness, the things that deeply impressed themselves into my mind and heart were the crib, the cross and the Mass. I remember the crib at Christmas time, assembled in the open space before the Lady altar, all straw and animals and cosiness. The message is powerful and clear: God is a God of tenderness who comes among us, born a child in Bethlehem. I knew all about tenderness, for we were always embraced and hugged and kissed at home. This is God's love, brought home to me literally in my own home, and shown to me at Christmas in a manger full of hay.

The cross of Jesus, which we celebrated every year in Holy Week, told me that God does not hide from the harsh realities of this world. As a child, I would always puzzle over the fact of suffering and the fact of unhappiness. Why do these horrible things have to be? But no matter that I could not find any answers to those tormenting issues, I knew that Jesus went through all the suffering that any person can go through. We prayed the sorrowful mysteries of the rosary, and every season of Lent we walked round the walls of the church, to think about the story of our Lord's walk to Calvary, in the devotion called *The Stations of the Cross.* So I knew that sad things would not have the last word in life, because of the joy of Easter and the resurrection of the Lord from the dead.

The Mass told me that Jesus comes right into my life and shares his life with mine. When I was a child, it was the red sanctuary lamp, shining on the wall and reminding me of the 'real presence' of the Lord as the bread of life, that warmed my heart to the nearness of God.

These three realities – crib, cross and Mass – were surrounded, then, by experiences of people together, flowers, candles and music. These experiences and this religion became my passport into the world, and my key for understanding the world.

With the passing years, it is the person of Jesus, as I have come to know him, that impresses me most. The gospel story, the stories that Jesus told, the conduct of the man himself in all his human circumstances, the promises he makes to us, the revealing of everlasting life. All these things make sense to me. And I have talked to the Lord all my life.

I have never, ever doubted Jesus Christ. The faith I have must be a gift to me, for I have done nothing to deserve it. It is given to me to use for the benefit of others I may meet. It is not a private luxury. But I do not spout religion. Like anyone in this world, I try to live a good life. I am very taken with Saint Paul's observation that 'faith is not given to everyone' (2 Thessalonians 3:2). Not everyone needs it. What is given to everyone is our human nature, imprinted on which we find the drive to live truly and justly, and to love kindly. We all have that. No one has any advantage over anyone else in our nature.

In my own story, the central struggle was for personal independence, for my own authority over my own life and destiny. The experience has taught me how careful we must be in nurturing our children into their adult years. Whenever I see stubborn wilfulness now in a child, I cheer inwardly and thank God to see such determination in such a little one. Checking a child is one thing. Suppressing their spirit is quite another.

This reminds me of a story that took place right outside my own house when I was 9 or 10. Another boy had provoked me into a fight on the grass in front of our house. My mother was informed and came out, thinking to stop the fight. My dad said to her, 'Leave him be, Eileen, or you might break his spirit.' How wise my father was! For, in my life, it has been the suppression of my spirit that proved the path of suffering for me. Being allowed to fight my own battle became the issue for me.

As a child, I found my local parish church to be very much like a large family. We lived a common life in that little Lancashire coalmining, cotton-mill town. There was great strength and human solidarity to be had there, in church and Mass and benediction, in school and sport and play. And although we were conscious of Christian divisions, they did not loom large or cause any problems for youngsters growing up then.

But I have one particular memory about Catholics and Protestants that has never left me. I was 10 years old, I guess, and was talking one day to a friend, John Wintle. Having been told all about Henry VIII and the wrong that he did, I found myself telling John, who was Protestant and attended a different school, how the Catholics were right and the Protestants were wrong. John did not have the ammunition to fight back against this historical salvo, and I can see him now, turning away in sadness and going across the road to his house.

As he went, I had the distinct feeling that something bad had just taken place. My religious knowledge had just caused a rift to develop between me and my friend. It left a sour taste in my mouth. Today I can see and can say that right and wrong are not so easily divided, and that John and I are quite simply children of a broken home, the fractured Christian Church.

Over in Ireland, down in my mother's Glen, I found another great family to belong to – the Carey clan. I also came to know a song that belonged very much to that place and to those people, and so also, a song that belongs to me. It was written by a native of the Glen – one Thomas McManamon, known as 'the poet' – and the song he wrote is called 'Down By Glencullen Side'. The warmth of this song impressed upon my growing mind a love of the place and a deep belief in the value of every human life and every human story. The song sings of a heartfelt love of the place, of a heartfelt longing for the place, and of a heartfelt love of the people of the place. It is a song of the joys and sorrows of life, and it really yearns for the day when all tears will be wiped away from all eyes.

My Aunt Sarah sang this song all her life, and she could sing it!

> O God be with the bygone days when, youthful,
> I did roam
> down by Glencullen's flowery braes beside my
> native home.
> Here silver dells and fields so green and moorland
> broad and wide
> and tranquil lakes that can be seen down by
> Glencullen side.

The song, like any good Irish song, goes on for many verses, for there are many things to tell of. We would all sit in hushed silence as Sarah's voice soared like a lark to tell of that beloved land. A poor land, yes, but so rich in people.

> Alas, I fear those days are gone, we never shall see
> them more,
> when free from care we boated on the Lake of
> Carrowmore.
> Alas, from home we had to go across the surging tide
> and bid farewell to all we knew and to Glencullen side.

The scattering of our clan that took place when our parents went to England, leaving only a few people still in the Glen, was healed by the gathering of the clan that took place on that August weekend in 2012. We are now a reunited people. Internet and email play a great part, but it was the gathering, the pilgrimage we all made back to the place where it all began, that now heals the sadness that took our parents away. What joy there would have been in heaven that day among our forebears, to see their children reunited and rejoicing in each other's company, down by Glencullen side!

There is a silent presence in my life that I also wish to acknowledge: the presence of my father. In the course of my life, especially in my young days, Daddy would leave things, in the main, to Mammy. That was the way of things in those days. It was in later years, sitting having a pint with him, for instance, that I got to talk to him more, and he was an easy man to be with. But his greatest influence on my life was not anything he said – although he did put it into words as I now recall – but simply the way he was. He was an honest man. He was a kind man. He stood up for justice, and, as he said to me one time, there is nothing more important in life than 'being proper with people'.

This lovely word – proper – holds within it a world of meaning. It stands for being proper in yourself – that is, honest and upright – and it stands for the relationship of truthfulness and consideration that should mark our connection to one another. In his own wise Lancashire way, my father was expressing the two great commandments of the law, the two commandments that are embedded in our very nature, in the way that God has made us. And the word he used was 'proper'.

When my life hit crisis over priesthood and the love of Maggie, another guiding spirit came into my world, that of the Irish writer John McGahern. If you read his books, you will see how he slowly and gradually removes from his system the oppressive and compacted cruelty that his father's tormented behaviours drove into his soul. Compacted ground is very hard to loosen, and I think that is McGahern's story – the gradual unearthing of compacted cruelty. As his life blossoms in later years, so his soul is free, and his final writings exhibit a happy and settled mind and heart. His final novel, *That They May Face The Rising Sun*, is a gentle, easy story. And his *Memoir* is his final word of love addressed to his beloved mother.

I found tremendous parallels of this story in my own life. The happy boy that I was, full of initiative and play, became, through long years in seminary, a rootless, de-energised, spiritless religious product. The spirit for life was knocked out of me in the process that formed me into a priest and put me into black clerical dress. The long years of that process made of my soul a compacted ground. Loosening up such a soul would not prove to be easy. To think that Maggie waited for me for seven years is, from one point of view, unacceptable to an outside observer. It sometimes makes me shake my head in wonderment. But as I try to understand how it could have taken so long for me to come to the light and to the day of freedom, I find explanations in my biddable, obedient nature, in my lack of rebelliousness or spirit, and in the deadening of my spirit that happened to me through 13 years of seminary existence.

McGahern says there is a liberation to be found in being able to understand your own story. When you look at what happened to you and how you were at the time, and how other people were, when you can explain the story to yourself, then it no longer holds you in its power. You are not a victim of that story any more. You have become the liver of your life. That is where I am today.

In this review of the guiding spirits who met me on the road of life, pride of place goes to Maggie, the girl I met and fell in love with, the girl who brought our son into the world, the girl who waited for me and who always challenged me healthily, the girl who willingly married me, the girl who made me so completely happy. Maggie never put pressure on me in any way. She was so patient. She seemed to know that if I was going to come out of the priesthood, I was the one who had to make that decision. I had to know for myself that it was what I wanted to do. I had to be free. But she was not soft with me either. If I said or thought something that did not make sense to her, she told me so. It is only now, now that she is gone from me, that I look back and say, 'How on earth did you put up with my indecision for so long?!' And that isn't a question!

My son, Michael, when writing his speech for his mum's funeral, made reference to 'my dad's indecision'. 'Is that all right? You don't mind me saying that, do you?' he checked with me.

'No,' I smiled, in complete recognition of the accuracy of his words. That is why, in my own final words at the end of the Requiem Mass, I told the assembled congregation, 'I would like to say that for the past 22 years of my life, Margaret has just loved me, loved me. Aren't I the lucky man?!' Indeed I am.

When Maggie died, so suddenly and so unexpectedly, my cousin Raymond said to me, 'You've been dealt a cruel hand, Brian.' There was indeed a truth in that, and it was a compassionate sentiment from a kind and loving cousin. But another truth tells me how fortunate a man I have been, in meeting Maggie and in being loved by her and allowed to love her as I did. The kind hand and the cruel hand come to all of us sooner or later. If we take joy from the hand of the Lord, must we not take sorrow too? That was Job's comment on the troubles of life, and it is a humble one. But it is not the last word, and I have never felt drawn to it or particularly consoled by it.

Rather, it is the Lord who consoles me. 'I am the resurrection and the life. He who believes in me will never die' (John 11:25).

Just after writing the above, I found myself on my Michael's Facebook page. At the foot of the page there is a place for entering your favourite quotes. I remember that in his final year at St Modan's High School here in Stirling, Michael studied the works of John Donne in the company of the then headmaster, Mr Francis Lennon. He really enjoyed that experience, and now here on his Facebook page I found these words, so well spoken by that Elizabethan poet–priest.

Death be not proud, though some have called thee Mighty and dreadful, for thou art not so.[8]

During the Requiem Mass that we celebrated for Maggie, Ed, in his sermon, quoted a story that I had told him in earlier days. As I struggled to sort out my life, one evening on the phone I said to Maggie, 'Maggie, you are the best thing that ever happened to me.'

---

8. John Donne, 'Death be not proud' (c.1610).

Immediately Maggie shot back at me, 'What do you mean "happened"? I'm still happening!'

Yes, you are, Maggie. You are still happening. And with all the saints in heaven, you are still my guiding light.

THIRTEEN

The view from here

I stand at the age of 66, one-time priest, Elvis lookalike, faithful Bolton supporter, Ireland-loving Lancashire boy. I lost my beloved wife a few months ago to a sudden and unexpected death, so I am now a widower. I feel the loneliness of that – these are desert days – but I am also a contented man, a happy man, with no complaints at all.

In the days of my life I have been many things: happy boy, promising footballer, clever, good at sport, top grader at Greek A level in 1964 – it's about time I boasted about that! I have been at boarding school (junior seminary), I was lost in Shropshire for six years and nobody knew I was lost (senior seminary). I was clothed in a black clerical suit as a Catholic priest. It always felt like prison garb to me. I never liked to wear it. I rebelled inwardly whenever I was reminded that I was one of the 'clergy'. I could not abide that word!

One day I walked free and came to Maggie and to Michael. We had some happy years together, 13 in all. They were not without worry, but they were happy all the same. Then Maggie died. Suddenly, in the blinking of an eye, my life was totally changed. A headache turned out to be a cerebral tumour, and within a matter of 24 hours, my beautiful wife had died.

I sit here now, nearly five months after her passing, and I look at the line of my life. It has been an interesting journey – I can see that now, and I can say it now. But there was a time – a long time – when I felt that my life was an unlived, unexpressed, derailed nothingness. A sorry tale indeed. Something whispered in a corner when it should have shouted to the hills.

I could blame people. I could blame the Church. Some people might tell me to blame myself. There would be some truth in all such accusations, but it would not help anyone to proceed like that. For when we are accused, we naturally seek to defend ourselves. And blame, like pointed arrows, fired with force, only succeeds at what it aims to do – hurt and wound another.

Far better to name things. Far better to tell a story and to describe things so that people may listen and watch and understand for themselves. Isn't that the way of Jesus? Telling stories, parables, which then speak for themselves, showing up our foolishness and leading us to simpler wisdoms.

We change through the course of our life. Cardinal Newman's words come to mind. 'To live is to change, and to be perfect is to have changed often.'[9] In those far-off childhood days, I used to accompany my mum to the 'Novena', a devotion to Our Lady, the mother of Jesus, brought to the parish by the Redemptorists, whom I was soon to join. Kneeling beside her in church, in our little church in Hindsford, I would hear her utter the words of a prayer asking for Our Lady's protection 'through all the changes of our journey through life.' It was a phrase that would rise to our lips many times in the course of the coming years.

In the pre-Vatican II years of Catholic pomp and certainty, years of many vocations, the Church had developed a policy of recruiting boys as young as 11, after they had

---

9. John Henry Newman, 'An Essay on the Development of Doctrine' (1845).

finished in primary school. As I see it now from a distance of years, this recruiting policy is geared to keep the flow of trainees high, so as to be able to fill all the positions that the growing Church required. The mindset was focused narrowly on the Church and the recruit. You show interest, we take you.

This policy failed completely to see all the natural relationships of life that it was severing. I lost real contact with my mother, my father, my two sisters, my brother, my dog, my friends, my local town and society. And I lost contact completely with girls. They were now off limits. It was unspoken but understood that the life I had embarked upon was down a particularly strict and narrowly defined road.

There come to mind now pictures on walls in so many Catholic presbyteries that I visited as a mission priest – pictures of the faces of a year group of priests, often as many as 40 faces in one frame. These were groups sent out from Maynooth or from other big colleges in Ireland, to all parts of the world, many to the United States. Today it makes me think of factory farming.

I used to stand before these photographs and wonder, 'Where are they now?' Or, more to the point, 'How are they now?' Some would be doing fine; others would have succumbed to one or both of the dangers that brought clergy down: Punch or Judy – drink or women. Or, perhaps nearer the point, loneliness, which might lead to Punch and/or Judy.

That whole way of life is ending now, though some like to think that it is not. The system established 500 years ago by the Council of Trent has served its time. A civil service of celibate priesthood has been and come and is almost gone. The Church historian, Eamon Duffy, has written well on this matter in his book, *Faith of Our Fathers*. There he says:

> The Tridentine moment is passing, perhaps has already passed . . . We need also to understand that the Tridentine vision is slowly but surely collapsing under the joint pressures of theological and social change. Without Tridentine structures and attitudes, we cannot have Tridentine priesthood.

At the close of the same chapter, chapter 11, in which he considers priesthood in the Church, Duffy ends with these words:

> As society changes, as the Church calls on all the laity to claim and exercise their priesthood, and as we discover that the charisms which help form the life of the Church can be given to all and not just to the clergy, we are confronted with an urgent need to reimagine the ordained priesthood.[10]

A different way of being Church lies ahead.

In the days of my childhood, if anyone showed any interest in Jesus and his Church they would be pointed towards priesthood and religious life. That is not the case today. This is a different world and, very slowly, it is becoming a different Church.

The change that came over the Church in the 1960s was earth shaking, and probably long overdue. I went away from home in 1958 when the Church was still led by the

---

10. Eamon Duffy, *Faith of Our Fathers*, (London and New York: Continuum, 2004), p.98-106.

ascetic-looking Pius XII, who held all the reins in his hands. With his death, the old world died, and up stepped John XXIII, an interim candidate who proved to be anything but. He opened the windows and doors of the Church, and what a wind blew through! By the time I was 'let out' of the college system and into an ordinary parish and ordinary streets again, Latin had given way to English, silence had given way to noise, hymns and organ had given way to pop songs and guitars.

People experience the Church most of all in the Mass – in its liturgy, its way of worship – and that way was changed beyond all recognition. I remember a lady in Clapham who was beside herself with anger at the damage inflicted on her Sunday Mass by the coming of the vernacular and the modern way. What hit me most then was her anger, and I found myself trying to respond to that. That taught me how expressed anger is not a good vehicle for communication. People receive the blast of anger without the intelligence of the content. That lady's issue with the Mass was a genuine issue. She had very good points to make, and she felt helpless about it, but her anger did not help her cause.

Change in the way of worship was very much needed, so as to involve everyone more fully in worship instead of people being merely spectators. But the way in which change was introduced was often very painful. We were a people who knew nothing about change, and suddenly we were faced with many changes to get used to.

Beautiful music, and well-loved music, was often sacrificed, and the great wound was the loss of silence, in which prayer best resides. Our world of mass media communication – of radio, television and general noise –

now invaded the quietest recesses of the Church, and 'Peace be with you' became a long lost sigh of the heart.

In my young days as a priest, I was designated to look after the ten o'clock Mass which had become a 'Folk Mass'. I had a young group of children who sang wholeheartedly, and some young folk, of around 14 and 15 years of age, who played guitar very well. One boy, Stephen Mooney, could make a guitar talk! In that old Gothic church of St Mary's, Clapham, we led the ten o'clock Mass every Sunday.

This was not the quiet church of my earlier years, and yet it was popular, because the children who sang were so young and so lovely. I can see them now. It was a family Mass, and that is why it was popular. Children were centre stage. If it had been about folk music, it would have been rubbished early on – except for Steve Mooney's guitar playing.

The Mass that followed on from ours, at 11 o'clock, was a traditional sung Mass, with organ music and a handful of elderly ladies in the choir who sang in high voices. They were lovely people. The organist – Mr Wilson – was extremely good. They were continuing the practice of the ages, the old way, in an age that was rapidly changing.

The disjunction between the ten o'clock and 11 o'clock Masses said everything about the disjunctive change that came over the Church in those days. There was I, going around unplugging leads from electric points, and there were the old faithful, singing their way into heaven. I do believe one of those lovely old ladies was called Nellie Dean.

The group of children who gathered around me were like children of my own. I loved them. I remember Stella

Blair, the D'Arcy girls – Jacqueline and Caroline – Joanne Gonzalez, Andrea Doyle, Caroline McCaffrey and the guitarists Angela Contucci, Peter Wingrave, Kevin Scanlan and Steve Mooney. They were at that age of goodness, enthusiasm and simple happiness that precedes the troubled times of teenage years. I was only young myself, having been locked away in seminary for 13 years and never allowed to meet or be with girls.

As well as inheriting a youth group for Mass, I inherited from a previous curate a new venture of running Irish dances in the parish hall. We had a grand sized hall, designed in the 1930s by an architect by the name of Fahy. I had to learn how to organise these events, ordering beer and spirits from a local brewery as well as a portable bar for the occasion. Once, when ordering soda water, I was asked by the girl at the brewery office, 'Is that splits or siphons?' I hadn't a clue what splits were, but I recognised a siphon, so on the night of the dance there were no splits to put in the drinks, but you could siphon away to your heart's content!

Many good bands came to our hall, and many good nights were enjoyed, dancing and socialising to Irish and country music. These became important moments in my life, for I connected so powerfully with music, with Ireland, and with all the people in the place. I was, I now realise, living something of my teenage years and energy ten years after its time. But I was always a good boy.

The third string to my bow in those days, after folk Mass and Irish dances, was football. I had always been a very good footballer, and now I played for a team called Clapham Harps. I was in my late twenties now and not as fit as I might have been, but for three seasons I played on such auspicious venues as Clapham Common, Tooting Common, Mitcham Common and Morden. All that area of south London became familiar to me, and Saturday afternoons were happy times.

I was dressed in black and working officially as a priest, but in truth, I was unconsciously working out of my system, or maybe into my system, the natural enthusiasms of youth that had been blocked in my seminary days. Not surprising, then, that the next thing to happen to me was to fall in love!

Life in the Church since the 1960s has been a painfully slow process of change. In fact, it has been a case of watching an old way dying while a new one is still coming to birth. People do not change easily, and when a new blueprint is put before us we need help from those who understand the vision. We need agents of change, and they were in short supply.

The principle agents of change would normally be the priests, but the priests were all trained in the old ways and in the old values. They were now the parish priests, and many would be set in their ways. It was almost unfair, and certainly unrealistic, to look to these men to lead the people into the new ways. Even now, the changes that are envisaged are huge, especially concerning the role of lay people in the Church. Things take as long as they take, and that is proving to be a painfully slow process for the Catholic Church in the West. Yes, 'Each age is a dream that is dying, or one that is coming to birth.'[11]

Sorting the world out, or in this case the Church, is sometimes a luxury best indulged in over a pint. The day

---

11. 'Ode', Arthur O'Shaughnessy (1874).

itself always brings more immediate issues before us, and how we live with one another is always our daily task. Since coming to Stirling I have spent ten years in the work of family mediation, and this experience has brought me face to face with the upsets, heartbreaks and angers of people who are struggling with the breakdown of relationships and with the need to care for or even to have contact with their children.

The kind of society that we have developed does not seem to help us in any way to sustain our relationships of love and family life. The social support that we all need is often lacking, and people find themselves working hard and being busy, but feeling on their own. The pervading philosophy of life that encourages people to pursue individual happiness as the main driver of their efforts surely sends people down many false avenues and foolish ways. Not only do we need to be converted to God, in the sense of turning our face towards the pursuit of goodness, but we also need to be converted every day towards one another, to turn our faces towards one another in the pursuit of kindness and loving service.

At the heart of our lives stands the person of Jesus, the crucified and living Lord. His Spirit, given to us to live in us, calls us to this way of life. Every day the Lord calls us to follow him.

I have always been very wary of the sentence in the American Constitution that speaks about 'the pursuit of happiness'. I fear that this sentence is too easily received as counsel for pursuing self-interest before all else. Happiness is the grace of God that comes to us when we pursue other things, namely justice, truthfulness, kindness and love of others. 'The pursuit of happiness', written by

Thomas Jefferson into the Constitution of the United States, is always in need of healthy interpretations.

The greatest people in this world are not those who make loud noises or who cut dramatic swathes through society. Rather, it is the capacity for others that makes the big difference in life. People who have time and attention for others, people who listen and seek to understand, people who by their very presence affirm the other in their own self – these are the truly great ones of our world.

One day, a girl I had known from my days in Clapham – Caroline McCaffrey – paid me a beautiful compliment. 'My little sister has great time for you,' she told me. Many years had gone by at this time.

'Why is that?' I asked.

'Because when she was small, she used to sit on your knee after Mass and ask you questions, and you always spoke to her properly, and not as if she was a baby.' Out of the mouths of babes . . .

My great hero in life is and has always been Jesus of Nazareth. Read his life story. Read of his dealings with other people – the things he said, the things he taught, the things he did. He was a man of God and a man for others. Silence and contemplation, kindness of conversation, wisdom and honesty marked his every word and movement. To be like him by asking for his grace to follow him, that has been the desire of my life. Nobody comes anywhere near him, and yet he calls everyone to draw near.

Since my Maggie died, I have been busy in business and busy in writing, as now, but I am also struggling to find 'a way to live', struggling to find the right attitude and intention with which to set out on the journey of daily life. I do not wish merely to be at the mercy of my moods, nor do I wish to have no agenda or purpose to my living days. I could so easily allow myself to be washed this way and that by every wave of feeling that comes over me, and those feelings would tend to be negative ones, sad ones. I need to address this state of affairs and make a better shift of things. I can hear Maggie telling me to do exactly that! The greatest love I can show for Maggie now is to be everything I am capable of being in the matters of self-discipline, kindness and consideration for others.

Maggie was like that. Everyone said she was. She lived for others. She cared about others. She attended to others. She greeted people. She was kind to every person who came to her door. She even called them 'darling'! Whenever I praised her for something she did, Maggie would say to me, 'Thank you very much. I'll send you the bill.' I could never pay the bill for all that I owe to Maggie, but I hope that in these written words I have paid a good tribute to her, and I thank God for the gift of Maggie that came so quietly and so gently into my life.

Afterword

On the day of my ordination to priesthood, an elderly couple had travelled from Ireland to be present on such an auspicious day in the life of my mother. Their names were Michael and Maria Devanney. They were Mayo people, like my mother. Maria was a sister of Jackie Walsh, who was married to my mother's eldest sister, Mary. Before the Second World War they were living in Manchester, and it was to their house that my mother, and her sisters before her, travelled when they began the great adventure of emigration. Their house was the anchor and the safe house for the girls leaving home. At the outbreak of war, Michael and Maria returned to Ireland, to Mayo, and to a quiet cottage on the banks of the River Moy.

One lovely afternoon of holidays in Ireland, with my mother and father and my young brother Michael, 12 months after my ordination, we returned the compliment to that elderly couple, and went to visit them in their faraway corner of Mayo. They lived not far from the village of Straide, the home of the great nineteenth-century Land League campaigner Michael Davitt. We drove by car as far as the car could go and, parking where the boreen became more or less a field, we walked the final stretch down to the cottage by the riverbank.

We received a great welcome from the elderly people, now well into their seventies, as we entered their two-roomed abode with its whitewashed walls and small windows. I sat before an open hearth of turf fire. To my left was a 'colic' – a settle bed beside the hearth. As we sat there and talked, suddenly the whole room went dark. I turned round to see what had caused this sudden darkening, and I saw that my father had gone to stand in the doorway. In doing so, he had blocked out all the light that came into the house. It was then that I understood, as for the first time, the meaning of the phrase, 'He hasn't darkened my doorway from that day to this.'

I now knew I was back among the origins of things, among my native people. After all those years in the wild wastes of college, here was warmth and ease and welcome, and a world that I always felt was mine. It was my mother's place, and one generation on, it was my father's place, and now it was my place again. Emigration took them away. Now I was coming home.

On the day of my ordination, back in 1970, as we climbed into the buses to take us home to Lancashire, the bus driver said to me as I climbed up into the coach, 'Well, Father Brian, what is it like to be a 'father' and not married?' I think he was waiting for me! I laughed at the joke and enjoyed it – a typical Lancashire working-class wisecrack! People liked to keep everybody on the same level, and I love that. If anyone tried to act superior, they would say in Lancashire, 'She's a bit peas above sticks!' Or if pregnancy came before marriage – not an uncommon occurrence – folk would say, 'Well, she put Monday before Sunday!'

I was a father and not married for many years, and then, eventually, I indeed became a father, and then I got married. I can tell the bus driver now that it is grand. On that day of ordination back in Shropshire, the two roots of my life – Lancashire and Mayo – were well represented in that wisecracking Lancashire bus driver and in the elderly couple from Mayo, sitting quietly in their seats on the bus. This story I have shared with you brings both sides together.

There was one other elderly gentleman sitting on the bus that day, by the name of Thomas Trumble. He was my father's uncle, a brother of my grandmother, Maggie Trumble. He was my connection with the First World War, as he had been a soldier in that terrible time. Two of his brothers, John and Owen, also fought, and they died in that war. I first heard about them when I was told stories that they had been sent to the 'naughty school' in Manchester as young boys, and that my grandmother, herself only a young girl, used to visit them and take them parcels.

Their mother had died when they were small, aged 10 and 9, and they must have become unruly through that emotional trauma. So off to the remand home they went. When war broke out they joined up. John died in Flanders in May 1916, and Owen met his death in Mesopotamia at Christmas 1917. Their names are inscribed on the war memorial in Tyldesley cemetery. I see them there every time I visit my father's grave. What life did they have?! What sorrow they endured! My own father could have joined them in a soldier's grave, but he was luckier than they. And in my own life, I did not endure anything like the hardship that my father had.

Now, as I am privileged to write these pages, and for these pages to see the light of day, I think it only right to place their names upon the page, and so to honour them – Owen and John Trumble – and in honouring them, 100 years on from that terrible slaughter, to honour all of their generation who, as the song says, 'were butchered and damned'.[12] May they rest in peace, and let perpetual light shine upon them now.

And the reason I wrote all this? Maggie. My beloved Maggie. She told me to. After she died, so suddenly and so unexpectedly, I received a letter from Anne Carey in Glencullen, the wife of my cousin Michael. She said to me that when talking to Maggie in the Glen, Maggie had said to her, 'Brian is good with words.' Hearing that reported conversation after her death, words carried back to me in a letter from the Glen, words that Maggie had spoken in the Glen, inspired me to go for it, to tell these stories, and to hope that in telling them I might bring light and joy into the lives of others, as Maggie brought light and joy into mine.

I hope I will write a lot more in my life. I want to be good with words. What else would you want to do with them?

---

12. Eric Bogle, 'The Green Fields of France', also known as 'No Man's Land' or 'Willie McBride', 1976.

Encore

In the months following the death of my wife, Margaret, I had no spirit for writing verse. The books, yes; the story, yes; but nothing poetic. Then one day in February, five months after my Maggie's death, two poems stirred inside me, asking to be written, and so here they are. One tells of the Mayo that I love. The second of the Maggie that I love. After the silence of longing and loss, my voice returns. I would like to share these poems with you.

Whatever places are dear to our hearts, whatever people are dear to us, let us treasure them, love them and celebrate them. In joy and in sorrow, in sunshine or in rain, we are on the one road. Let us walk the road together.

Mayo

The names of Mayo villages are floating through
my mind.
Bohola, Straide and Binghamstown and others of
their kind
come floating on this evening air as I sit here and stare
and wander back among my dreams and memories
so rare.

I am an emigrant, you see, a man from far away.
It wasn't I that left those shores on that far distant day.
My mother was the one to roam across the foreign sea.
And my father, though an Englishman, was as Irish as
can be.

His Daddy came from Kilmaclasser, from Slinaun,
as I know.

I've been to see his homestead in that County of Mayo.
That house is now enlarged and grand, its occupants
are fine.
The family that had once lived there, their memory is
all mine.

I wander back because I yearn for the taste of yesteryear.
I want to see and feel again those memories so dear
of people and of places that filled my heart with joy
and made my life so wonderful when I was still a boy.

In England I have lived my life, though Scotland holds
me now.
But Ireland was my paradise, my promise and my vow.
And Mayo was my always dream, the place I longed
for most,
and in all my earthly travelling it was my proudest boast.

I know that life in 'real' Mayo is a struggle and a test.
As it is in any other place, you have to do your best.
But for me it means so much besides, not easy to explain.
It is my home, my everything, in sunshine and in rain.

I came here every year, you see, as though
returning home.
We loved that journey, though so long, across the
churning foam.
We came to claim our origins, to place our foot once more
upon the soil that we called home by the lake
of Carrowmore.

Glencullen was our real true home, we knew it from
the start.
The house, the hills, the children, were places in
our heart.

We were not strangers, never, we arrived and just filled in.
Our cousins took us to their hearts as if we had
always been.

So now I turn and look again at that long distant scene,
and I know my childhood was enriched beyond any
'might have been'.
I reaped the harvest of true love in a family so fine,
and I cannot thank the Lord enough for the childhood
that was mine.

Margaret

Your lovely face is what I saw
the day you came to call.
And people gathered round you,
already in your thrall.

That girl is mine, I told myself,
it is me she has come to see.
And we made a time to meet again
when I would be quite free.

We sat and talked in my wee room,
you told me all your story
And I tried to be your mirror,
reflecting back your glory.

A wrong word never passed your lips.
You did not deal in blame.
You unfolded life and set it free,
and for me you did the same.

From that chance meeting on the hill
my days in chains were numbered.
You showed me a freer way to walk
from the darkness where I slumbered.

And your face that time in hospital
when the surgeon's work was done
was a look I had never seen before
the ordeal and the sun.

Nobody ever looked at me
in quite the way you did,
for nobody ever knows so well
a heart forever hid.

Only the one who loves you so
and loves you till they die.
And that was you, my Maggie,
and that is why I cry.

And now your face looks out at me
from photos all around,
but the face I always want to see
lies now in sacred ground.

Your face I'll see again one day,
I know that and rejoice.
But these are days of grieving now,
days without a voice.

But truth to tell, my voice returns.
These words I write for you,
for you have been my one true love,
and payment is overdue.

I'll live the day and write away
and fill my life with longing.
But not the empty, lonely kind,
but the kind that's all belonging.

To try and be as you were here
in the days of your blessed living.
To live for others and find my joy
in the simple ways of giving.

'We must not ever let ourselves
be prisoners of sorrow,'
so Benedict says, and so I'll try
to face each new tomorrow.

You are my Margarita, girl,
the gemstone of my life.
My girl, my love, my only one,
my lovely darling wife.

Our Wedding Day, 16 October 2004

My mother, Ellen Carey, photo
taken in Manchester in the 1940s

My mother at her 90th birthday celebration in
Westport, Ireland, August 2006